THE EUCHARIST

THE

Eucharist
A View From the Pew

GERARD P. WEBER

ST. ANTHONY MESSENGER PRESS
Cincinnati, Ohio

Nihil Obstat: Rev. Thomas Richstatter, O.F.M.
Rev. Ralph J. Lawrence

Imprimi Potest: Rev. Fred Link, O.F.M.
Provincial

Imprimatur: +Most Rev. Carl K. Moeddel, V.G.
Archdiocese of Cincinnati
September 5, 2000

The *nihil obstat* and *imprimatur* are a declaration that a book is considered to be free from doctrinal or moral error. It is not implied that those who have granted the *nihil obstat* and *imprimatur* agree with the contents, opinions or statements expressed.

Cover design by Mary Alfieri
Cover photo (background) by Gene Plaisted, O.S.C.
Cover photo (inset) by Franciscan Communications/Edd Anthony
Book design by Sandy L. Digman

ISBN 0-86716-415-8
Published by St. Anthony Messenger Press
www.AmericanCatholic.org
Printed in the U.S.A.

CONTENTS

Preface

Much has been written about the manner in which the celebrant is to preside at the Eucharist. Practically every parish has had instruction classes and training courses for lay people who undertake the ministry of acolyte, lector, extraordinary minister of Communion or liturgical planner. There have also been clear directives about what the people in the pews are to *do* when they are at the Eucharist. However, there does not seem to be much material available about the ideas, interior sentiments and feelings which may help the people in the congregation participate more meaningfully.

I make no claim to be presenting a theological or liturgical study of the Mass. I am merely presenting some ideas and insights which have helped me share more fully in the movement of the Mass. I make no claim to authority in this matter, other than having spent more than seventy years in the pews or at the altar.

In my descriptions of what the people in the pews do during Mass I make no pretense of describing the correct way things should be done. I am merely describing what I have observed in various parishes around the country. I have no intention of initiating discussions about the right and the wrong way to stand, sit or pray. That is the responsibility of the bishop. However, I am interested in priming discussions about the meaning of the various prayers and actions of the eucharistic celebration, as well as surfacing people's thoughts and feelings about them.

As I work on this material I realize that in many ways I, too, sit in the pew day after day. Usually I am not the presiding priest. I am a concelebrant. It is true that I am on the altar, but I have little to say or do. My participation, like that of the people in the pews, is mostly what goes on in my head and heart as the various parts of the Mass unfold. I have no magical formula which will ensure the "conscious, active and full participation...motivated by faith, hope and charity" called for in the General Instruction of the Roman Missal in *The Sacramentary* (page 20, #3). Even though I still have trouble keeping my thoughts and feelings centered on what is occurring, I can share with you some of the ideas which over the years have helped me feel a part of what is being celebrated there.

This book is intended primarily for people who regularly attend the Eucharist and wish to grow closer to God. It was written with small groups in mind. The Discussion Starters are intended to kick off sharing and discussion after a section of the book has been read aloud in the group.

Up front I must thank the members of my Bible Study Group at Our Lady of Grace parish, as well as those in my small faith community at St. Mel's parish along with the ladies in the Monday morning and Thursday evening groups who were kind enough to discuss the first draft of this book and suggest changes and clarifications. Special thanks to Mark Hughes who suggested the direction the book should take and to Fathers Hilarion Kistner, O.F.M., and Thomas Richstatter, O.F.M., who were kind enough to offer a number of helpful suggestions after reading the manuscript.

Dedicated to Monsignor Reynold Hillenbrand, who as rector of St. Mary of the Lake Seminary, Mundelein, Illinois, first opened my eyes to the fact that liturgy was more than rubrics.

Gerard P. Weber
Encino, California, January 1, 2000

PART ONE

*The
Celebration
and the
Pew*

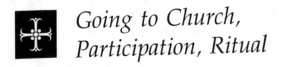

Going to Church, Participation, Ritual

A Voice From the Pew

One day sitting around a friend's kitchen table, we were discussing the reasons people have for regular participation in the Eucharist. We were commenting on the fact that today the fundamental question we need to ask is not why so many people no longer go to Mass, but why so many do attend regularly. Many have only a vague understanding of what is occurring and of how they are to participate. However, they realize in some way or other, that they are in touch with the divine.

I described my idea for a book to help these regular Mass-goers understand the basic structure of the Eucharist better and participate more fully. My host listened, said little and asked, "From what perspective—the preacher's, the teacher's or the person's in the pew?" Startled I replied, "The teacher's. That's what I am." He shook his head and responded, "Write it from the pew." I thought about his words and realized that he was right. There are many books from the viewpoint of teacher, priest or theologian, but very few from that of the people who sit in the pews Sunday after Sunday. I realized that I could not teach people how they should feel or respond to God at the Eucharist. These are always individual and conditioned by circumstances. I hope that some ideas on the responses called for by the various parts of the Mass will help the Sunday regulars get more out of being part of the eucharistic celebration. Nor do I expect the readers to be conscious of the ideas and sentiments I present every time they participate in the Eucharist. My only aim and hope is that at some celebration one or the other of these suggestions will enhance their manner of participating.

Going to Church

Every Sunday morning it is the same picture. Cars fill the parking lot. Families pour out of vans. The handicapped spots are filled. Adults amble or hurry as they make their way through the cars or along the sidewalk. Little children dance or cry as they are led or pulled along protesting all the time. We join the crowd. People around us are hurrying, trying not to be late. Teenagers cluster and meander slowly toward the doors of the church. Some of the latecomers will have been held up by traffic. Others will have spent precious minutes looking for a child's lost shoe or for the collection envelope that has been misplaced. In any case, by ten or fifteen minutes past the hour the parking lot will have quieted down.

If we would ask the people in this crowd where they were going, they would look at us as though we were total ignoramuses. "Of course! We are going to church!" If we press them and ask what they mean by the word "church," we will find that most people usually associate the word, "church," with a building. But the question then is, "What makes a building a church? Is it a certain type of architecture? Is it a sign in the window or hung over a door?" A church is a holy place where people gather to worship God. The building can be as simple as a rented hall in a local school or as ornate as Notre Dame in Paris. It can be as small as a windowless prison room holding only twenty men or as large as St. Peter's in Rome. It can be decorated in the best of taste or in the worst of taste. It could even be a field or a room in a house. The place is not as important as what occurs there.

What happens in such a place to make it holy? Is it because people have labeled it as a house of God? Is it because the bishop has blessed it? Is it because certain religious rites take place there? These are indications that a building has been set aside as a place dedicated to God, but its holiness comes not from the building itself. Its holiness comes from the fact that the holy People of God gather in it to pray and worship. It is important

4

to think of church as the congregation, the people called and gathered together by the Holy Spirit.

The same word, "church," is used when we speak about the building, about the congregation or even about the hierarchy. One thing is certain. Each of us hurrying through the parking lot has our personal understanding and feelings about all three meanings of the word "church." Some of these are profound and powerful, some pleasant or nostalgic, some may even be negative. All of these feelings and ideas will color the way we participate in the celebration of the Eucharist that is about to take place. (See Discussion Starters, page 16.)

However, when we look for ways to make our participation more meaningful and more helpful it is important to reflect on the different words we use to describe what we do in the church building which makes it holy. The various combinations of verbs and nouns all refer to the same reality, but each subtly implies a different level of participation on the part of us who sit in the pews. The verbs are "go," "attend," "participate," "celebrate." The nouns are the "Mass," the "Eucharist," the "liturgy." We say that we go to Mass, that we attend Mass. These sentences imply that the important thing is to be present for the ceremony called the Mass. The word "Mass" comes from the Latin, "*Ite missa est*" ("Go, it is ended"). This short sentence is the dismissal or end of the Latin Mass. This is not a very illuminating way of expressing what we have been doing. If we say that we go to the liturgy or the Eucharist, we have a better idea of what we are doing. In Greek the word "liturgy" roughly means "people at work at worship" and the word "Eucharist" means "thanksgiving." However, the verbs "go" and "attend" do not imply what we are to do when we get there.

Not too many years ago we would say that for one to hear Mass it was only necessary to be present for the Offertory, the Consecration and the Communion. Nothing was said about the part we played, other than being there and contributing to the collection. More involvement is implied if we say that we celebrate or participate in the Eucharist or the liturgy. These combinations of verbs and nouns imply that we have an active role in giving thanks or in doing the work of worship.

In the following pages I will use these various verbs and

nouns interchangeably to help people who are used to saying that they are going to Mass become familiar with other ways of expressing what they are doing.

However, the celebration we speak of is not the same as a birthday or an anniversary party that simply recalls an event from the past. This celebration is a special type of religious celebration in which a past remembered event becomes present to us. This remembered event is the life, death, resurrection and ascension of Jesus, which conquered sin and death. We use the phrase "Pascal Mystery" to encompass all these events, because the death and resurrection of Jesus occurred at Passover time. We say it is a mystery because the words and actions point to the hidden but powerful presence of God. Through them in a unique, dynamic and mysterious way God's love reaches through time and space to embrace us as beloved sons and daughters. We do not understand how the liberating victory of Jesus' death nor how God's overwhelming love become present at our altar. Faith tells us it is so. (See Discussion Starters, page 16.)

What Do We Expect?

Being involved in celebrating or remembering such a fantastic event obviously calls us to be present in mind and heart as well as in word, action and song. But how we are actually present will depend on what we are looking for in the eucharistic celebration. I think that most regular attendees are looking for something more than a feeling of satisfaction that they are giving back to God an hour out of the 168 hours he has given them in the past week. They are seeking more than a sense of relief that once again they have avoided a mortal sin by fulfilling their Sunday obligation. I think that most of us would like something more than merely a feeling that somehow we are in touch with God. I think we would like to be present and to participate in this wondrous action in a way that changes us for the better, in a way that brings us into a living, vital relationship with the Trinity. We would like to be encouraged and inspired. We hunger for a good homily that speaks to our lives. We may like to hear inspiring music or even the old Latin Mass. We also may like to have more quiet in the church and to be able to see and hear what is going on.

However, the fulfillment of most of these expectations depends in great part on what someone else does. If we expect the priest and the other ministers to carry the entire burden of actively involving us in the Mass, we can often expect to be disappointed. If we expect the priest to preach a soul-searing homily every Sunday we will often be dissatisfied. If we expect the music to touch our hearts and to raise our thoughts to heaven, we may not hear it at our parish. The people in the pews have little control over the way the liturgy is performed. We cannot depend on what others do to meet our expectations. They may or may not help us enter body and soul, mind and heart into the celebration of the liturgy. It is what the Lord does and the way we personally open ourselves to God's action that will make the Mass come alive for us.

What we expect from the Mass is one thing. What the Lord is offering us is a much different matter. In the poetic language of the Scriptures, he is offering us a place at the banquet, everlasting life. The gift of this new life, of forgiveness of sins and salvation, does not depend on how well the ceremonies are performed nor on what we do. It is always freely offered to us by God. The only thing required of us is that we accept what is laid before us. One priest pictured it this way. If we stand with our hands cupped, God will fill them. If we stand with our arms outstretched, God will fill them to overflowing. The manner in which we take part in the Eucharist is our way of showing God that our hearts are open to receive whatever he is more than willing to give. If this is so, we may need to examine how we feel about going to church and clarify our understanding of the liturgy and of participation. (See Discussion Starters, page 16.)

Feelings and Ideas About Participation

Our feelings dictate to a great degree how we approach something we are about to do. If we have very positive feelings about celebrating the liturgy, we will look forward to the Sunday or daily Eucharist. We will be reaching out to receive the gift the Lord is offering. We will concentrate on the prayers and on the activity at the altar. We will make the extra effort necessary to attend. If we do not succeed in getting there something will seem to be missing from our day. People with a love for the Mass always seem to have worked out a way to take part in what is occurring at the altar.

If we are not sure what the liturgy is all about or whether it is the focal point of our contact with the Lord, we will have ambivalent feelings about the Lord's offer. Our response to his offer will be tentative or half-hearted. We will attend, but the ritual will have little meaning or impact. Our participation will be mostly superficial. We may sing, pray, sit or stand at the proper time, but we will not put our whole heart and soul into what we are doing.

Finally, if we do not anticipate getting anything out of the liturgy, if we feel resentment because as children we were forced to attend or if we anticipate being bored, our attitude will be a negative one. In effect we will be brushing aside the gift being set before us even before it is offered. The ritual and the poetry of the language will have no impact on us. We will seldom, if ever, participate in any way, shape or form.

Whatever we desire or expect from the liturgy, our expectation is grounded in the way we see that which cannot be seen and hear that which cannot be heard. Once we step through the door of the church building we are entering the world of the mysterious, mystical action of God in the lives of his people throughout history. It is mysterious because we cannot see or hear or feel the loving action of God. We can understand how the ceremonies of the Eucharist have evolved and changed over the centuries. We can grasp the meaning of the prayers and be inspired by the music. But the core reality of God reaching out to us and embracing us with the love he has for his Son, Jesus the Christ, can be grasped only through faith.

The Mass is a mystical action because it is the preeminent means by which we are put into contact with God through the mediation of Christ. In a mysterious manner beyond our comprehension we become present to Christ's life, death, resurrection and ascension. He invites us to his banquet table and unites us to his loving sacrifice on the cross. He feeds us with the food of himself to nourish the life he shares with us through Baptism.

For centuries theologians have struggled to explain how this mind-boggling, continuing, redemptive act occurs. Ultimately, the answer is, "By the mysterious power of the God in whom there is no past, present or future, the God in whom all is as one."

Liturgy is a way we come to know the unknowable, see the unseeable and experience the untouchable. It is the action of the Holy Spirit drawing us into the saving activity of Jesus' life, death and resurrection. With this understanding of what liturgy is really about, we realize that instruction and inspiration are secondary. What is important on our part is opening our eyes and ears, our minds and hearts, to accept this gracious gift and to express our gratitude for it.

The liturgy is a public and group participation in the saving activity of God. This communal work requires us not only to open our hearts to the invisible action and power of God, but also to work with, to join with the others in offering glory and thanks to God. The things we do as a group help us as individuals tune in to the invisible melody of liberation and salvation God is playing out in creation.

Many of us have a very limited idea of what participation in this group worship entails. We may think that each one is expected to be doing something like reading or serving or distributing Communion. It is obvious that in any parish only a very few people will have these roles. We may think that singing together and reciting a few responses to the priest's prayers is all that is required of us. Participation is more than that. It involves every person in the church body and soul, mind and heart. We are invited to join in this great act of worship by making certain bodily gestures together. We stand, kneel or sit. We fold our hands or extend them in supplication. These actions, when done in unison, are an expression not only of our individual feelings, but also of those of the entire community. Actions and even thoughts often are most eloquently expressed by a simple gesture. Through the prayers we say, the gestures we make, the attitudes we have in our minds and the feelings we have in our hearts we actively participate along with the presiding priest in the remembering and making present the sacrifice of Christ until he comes once again in glory.

By the fact that we are present we are already participating. The question then is, "Is my participation only one of 'me and God' or is it one of 'we and God'?" Is it mostly individual or is it communal? If it is the first, we may think of the celebration of the liturgy as the background, the religious motif, for our private time of prayer with God. Any sort of external participation is a distraction. We do not feel comfortable being called to pray in unison with the rest of the community, of being asked to sing or join in a procession. We may feel that this is a quiet time for us to say our private prayers. If it is communal we realize that we are part of a community, the People of God, and that as a community we pay communal worship to the Lord that is different from our individual worship. For a time we set aside our beloved forms of private prayer and our favorite hymns for the prayers and songs of the community. We sing along with the voice God has given us and we echo in our minds and hearts the ideas and sentiments of the community's prayers.

Of course we realize that what is happening in our lives on a particular day will have an impact on how much heart and soul we can put into the songs we sing, the words we say, the gestures we make. Our participation also depends on our expectation of what the Mass is supposed to be for us as well as our understanding of our faith and of the nature of the Eucharist as sacrifice and banquet. I have found that the more I understand and appreciate the role of ritual and symbol in worship the more the Mass means to me. The more I have learned about the structure of the Mass and the meaning of its prayers the more they have come to mean to me. I have learned to concentrate on what I believe is actually occurring and less on the externals of people, place and ceremonies. The unseen reality is the loving redeeming activity of Jesus.

Most of us have experienced changes over the years in the way we think about the liturgy and participate in it. My thinking and feelings about it and my role as a participant have changed slowly over the years. I must admit that for many years I never thought much about how I was to participate. I knew when I was to stand, kneel or sit, but that was about it. From my earliest years I was taken to Mass on Sundays. I do not remember how I participated while I was in grade school. I expect that I squirmed and protested as most boys do. When I entered the preparatory seminary I was told that I was expected to attend Mass every day. Even though I lived at home during those five years, I did go to Mass each day without much thought or feeling. I would dash off at 6:45 a.m. to catch the 7 a.m. Mass. Participation meant that I would be physically present in the church while the priest was doing his thing. I would say the rosary, read a prayer book or missal, daydream or pray by myself. I had no sense of community with the others who were present and I certainly never thought that in some way I was involved in what was going on at the altar. At the major seminary I learned that the Mass was the center of the Christian life to which and from which all things flowed. I was not sure what that meant. Our rector encouraged us to participate actively in a very organized way. We had the recited Mass, a very innovative practice sixty odd years ago. We all made the responses which belonged to the altar boys. We stood and sang together. We joined in the Gloria and Creed and the *Agnus Dei*. I tried to make the prayers in the missal be my prayer. I was not too successful. I saw the Mass more as an act of faith and obedience. It was a way of telling God that I would do what was required and that I believed that in some way the sacrifice of Christ was being made present at the altar.

After ordination my external participation was easier. Now I said all the prayers and tried to lead the congregation to join in with the responses. Not many could or did. Most kept to their rosaries and prayer books. They did their thing and I did mine. When the altars were turned around after the Second Vatican Council, I gradually began to sense that participation was more than saying the correct words and performing the right actions at the right time. I sensed the obvious, that my soul and heart had to be united to what I did. A good part of the time I fail, but now and then the words I recite actually become my prayer and the actions I do have a deeper meaning for me.

Now I am retired. I help out at nearby parishes. On the days when I am not needed I concelebrate. I am not the main celebrant. I sit on the sidelines while another priest leads the prayers. I do join in at the Consecration and help distribute Communion. This vantage point puts me more in tune with what the people in the pews experience. My efforts to participate vary from day to day, depending on how I feel and what I am dealing with in my life. Most days I try to be deeply involved in what is occurring at the altar. I endeavor to center my thoughts on the reality of what is occurring. I struggle to make the sentiments in my heart match the words we say or sing. On these days the saying, "The Eucharist forms us as we are forming the Eucharist," makes sense to me. But there are other times when I am physically present, but mentally far away. My thoughts wander all over the place. I am distracted and concerned about other things. I say the words and go through the actions mechanically. I would imagine that something similar happens to others who attend Mass week after week. (See Discussion Starters, page 16.)

Participation Needs 'Soul'

People often say that they could understand the Mass better and participate more meaningfully if they knew more about how things are to be done and why they are being done. They say they want to understand what is going on. Understanding can be fostered by acquiring information. Church documents and scholarly books present an ideal of what the celebration of the Eucharist is supposed to produce in the minds and hearts of those who sit in the pews. They describe in detail the way the church should be decorated and the way the ceremonies are to be performed. Their message is lifeless if the people in the pews merely go through the motions without feeling and understanding. Knowledge and understanding in themselves will not ensure that the Eucharist will become the center of our spiritual lives. Something more is needed if the Eucharist is to be the keystone of our spiritual growth. To knowledge and understanding must be added "soul."

"Soul" is impossible to define. It can only be described by identifying some of the elements which put feeling and vitality into what is being done. The basic element of "soul" is a deep and joyful sense of thanksgiving that God is a good God who does great things for us. It requires a strong desire to be a part of this action of thanksgiving. "Soul" is fostered by a realization that together we make the liturgy and that the liturgy makes us strong Catholics. It is nourished by our understanding of the deeper meaning of what we are doing. It is an attitude which sees what we are doing as the most important thing in our day. It is fostered by reflection, prayer and experience. It helps us get into the spirit of the liturgy and participate with both mind and heart. For this reason it is possible to have "soul" even when our emotions are at a low ebb because "soul" flows from a living faith. (See Discussion Starters, page 16.)

Religious Ritual Carries Us Into Another World

Very often the reason we are given to explain people's negative attitude about the Eucharist is something to the effect that it is the same old thing over and over again, that it is boring. Maybe so; maybe not. It depends in great part on how well we understand and enter into the ritual being carried out before our eyes.

Ritual is the customary or the habitual words and actions used in a religious ceremony. We stand, sit, kneel and pray together in more or less the same prescribed way. Doing the same thing in the same way, time after time, can get boring if we do not appreciate the importance of habit, especially religious habits in our lives. Habits, especially good ones, free us from consciously making those thousands of little decisions we would have to make to be able to function each day. Just imagine what life would be like if we had to figure out each morning the importance of and purpose of washing our face, cleaning our teeth, putting on our clothes and finding food for breakfast and then every evening weighing the pros and cons, the short-term consequences and the long-term consequences of getting enough sleep. Most likely we would not finish the morning chores until it would be time for bed. Habits are routine which makes life tolerable and easier.

Formal religious habits, or rituals, do more than help us get through a task without too much thought. Subtle messages buried in them awaken us to the presence and activity of the invisible, hidden God. They free us to bring up feelings, memories and understandings which nourish our relationship with God. They give form to feelings, longings and even ideas which are difficult to put into words. The words we say or hear and the actions we do or see have an obvious meaning. If we hear and take to heart that message our participation will be more than purely mechanical and the Mass will have meaning for us. Of course, we cannot be conscious of all these unspoken messages each time we take part in the Eucharist. We can, however, be conscious at every Mass that there is a richness of ideas and feelings beyond that which we see or hear. By discovering these we can enrich our participation in the Eucharist. (See *Catechism of the Catholic Church*, #1145-1152.)

Religious rituals change slowly because they are the routine of a group and because of the centuries of memories and symbols buried in them. If there are too many changes or if they come too frequently, we spend our time figuring out what we are expected to do and why we are doing this or that, rather than allowing the prayers and action to guide us into union with God. Making frequent changes in words and ceremonies demands a very great amount of ingenuity. Often a person or a group will make changes so that the liturgy will be more relevant. Often enough those changes are repeated time and time again. They, too, become routine and others will say about them, "They're boring!"

Routine can become deadly if there is no variety in what is being said or done. Our present way of celebrating offers a good deal of variety. There are the liturgical seasons of Advent, Christmas, Lent, Easter and Ordinary Time. Each emphasizes a different aspect of the Lord's life. Each has a predominant theme. Each emphasizes a way for us to respond. This theme and this response is clear in the Scripture readings. It is also heard in the changeable prayers and the seasonal prefaces. Intertwined with seasons of the liturgical year are the special feasts of our Lord and our Lady, as well as the memorials of the saints.

Changes Over the Centuries

Changing times and circumstances do demand some change. Some people will clamor for radical changes in the set routine. Others will say, "This is the way it has always been done. This is the way it should be done!" Both of these cries need to be carefully examined when speaking about the celebration of the

Eucharist. The core cannot be changed because our Lord gave the Church a way to remember him. He took, blessed, broke and distributed the bread and did similarly with the wine. All else has changed and developed gradually in different ways in different lands and in different local churches. The Acts of the Apostles just hints at what the apostles and early Christians did. They gathered for a meal, blessed and broke bread, consumed the wine.

Shortly changes began to be made. The Eucharist was separated from the meal and a Scripture and prayer service was added. The manner in which the Eucharist was celebrated was left to the local leader. It was not more than a hundred years before routines or set rituals appeared. In time the differing ways of celebrating by bishops in major Churches such as Alexandria, Antioch, Constantinople and Rome were adopted by the surrounding Churches. Today some of the Churches which trace their roots to these ancient Churches are not in union with Rome. Others or sections of others are. However, the Church recognizes and respects eighteen variations or rites which have developed from these ancient Churches. They all use their own language and somewhat different ceremonies and prayers. All of them have readings from Scriptures and the essential action of Jesus who took, blessed, broke and distributed the lifegiving bread and wine at the Last Supper and told his disciples to do this in memory of him.

Of these various Catholic rites one is the Latin Rite, which developed in Rome and became the norm for the countries of the West and for any place that missionaries from the West went. But even in the West modifications and changes of actions and words have occurred over the centuries. For example, it was not so long ago that we had to fast from midnight before Communion, that the priests used the Latin language and were the only ones allowed to touch the host. Today we use English, fast but briefly. The lay people distribute Communion and have important roles at the Eucharist. These changes came gradually over the past forty years or so. Most likely more will come in the next forty. The way we celebrate the Eucharist will continue to change, but slowly. (See Discussion Starters, page 17.)

Time to Prepare

Liturgy like any other important action requires preparation. We cannot pop into church and immediately be in the mood to touch in with God. A good many people prepare during the preceding week. Alone or with a group they read and ponder the Scriptures for the coming Sunday. Some spend time each day in meditation or contemplation. Others do a bit of spiritual reading. On their way to church some try to collect their thoughts and think about what they are about to do. Several people have said that they do not turn on their car radios during this time. Most of us try to shift mental gears in the few minutes between entering the church, finding a seat, settling down and waiting for the priests and ministers to enter. We try to set aside the cares and concerns of daily life and open ourselves to the great mysterious and mystical action which is about to begin. (See Discussion Starters, page 17.)

DISCUSSION STARTERS

The sentences to be completed and the questions to be answered are meant to jump-start a discussion in the group about the material you have just read. They are not a test. Allow the discussion to flow.

- *What thoughts, images or feelings come to mind when you hear the word "church"?*

- *The words "participate" or "celebrate" suggest that we are to*

  _____.

- *In what way would you like the Mass to help you?*

- *In what way has your participation at the celebration of the Eucharist changed over the years?*

- *Describe a Mass you have taken part in that you feel had "soul."*

- *What effects have changes in the Mass over the past several years had on you?*

- *How do you prepare for the coming Sunday's Eucharist?*

PART TWO

*Introductory
Rites*

Entrance Song, Greeting, Blessing and Sprinkling With Holy Water, Penitential Rite, Gloria, Opening Prayer

We Enter the Realm of the Sacred

We hurry through the doors of the church. We quiet down. We dip our fingers into the holy water font and make the sign of the cross. We look for our usual pew to see whether someone may have usurped our place. We are following a routine established many years before and we do not think much about it. We say that we are coming to church, but is that all we are doing? By the simple action of stepping over the threshold we are entering a world rich in religious symbolism and beauty. This is a world where we see things that the eyes cannot see and hear things that the ears do not hear. It is a world whose language is metaphor, analogy, simile and, especially, poetry. This language is telling us something more meaningful, more powerful, more life-giving than words can adequately express. Symbols, poetry, figurative language suffer when we try to analyze them too closely. The most helpful thing is to try to catch what they are hinting at, to look beyond the obvious. This poetic and image-filled language is intended to open the doors of our hearts to God. It is intended to put "soul" into our presence and participation whether or not we say a word or perform a role.

The simple actions we do at the Eucharist can be understood

symbolically. As such they feed our sense of awe and wonder. Thus, we walk through the door. Simple enough—we want to get inside. But in reality we are responding to a personal invitation heard by our heart, not by our ears. Centuries ago it was expressed when Jesus said, "Ask and it will be given to you; seek and you will find; knock and the door will be opened to you" (Matthew 7:7). Figuratively we are knocking each time we come to the church door. We have come to seek and to ask. Sometimes what we seek and ask is very clear in our minds. At other times it is implied by the simple action of walking through the door. We are seeking to know and love God more. By stepping over the threshold we are assured that the door is open and that what we seek and ask for will be found.

We dip our fingers into the holy water font and make the sign of the cross. A split second of reflection will center our attention and focus our thoughts on who is opening the door to us. The Trinity is welcoming us. In this simple gesture, made too often in a hurried manner, we make a profound profession of faith. We are expressing the kind of God we believe in, three persons in one nature. We are praising the Father who created us, the Son who died for us on the cross and the Spirit who dwells within us. By blessing ourselves with holy water we are also reminding ourselves that through the waters of Baptism we were given a new and different kind of life. Like the Hebrews who crossed the waters of the Jordan to enter the Promised Land we are entering our new homeland. We are acknowledging that whatever we do during the next hour or so we will do with the power of the Trinity. The reverence with which we perform this simple ritual draws us into the loving, mysterious, powerful embrace of the one God who welcomes us to this Eucharist.

We find our pew, make a genuflection to the Blessed Sacrament, slide into the pew, drop to our knees, recite a short prayer and slide back onto the seat waiting for the Mass to begin. If the tabernacle is not visible, we make a bow to the cross. Both genuflecting and bowing were ancient signs of reverence and respect for important people, such as emperors and their officials. When genuflections were no longer considered a sign of adoration of the emperor who claimed to be god, they were introduced into the liturgy. By the thirteenth century they had become more than an act of reverence to the Lord Jesus. They had become an act of adoration, an act of faith in the real presence because some people were denying that Christ was really and truly present in the Eucharist. Genuflections have never been used in the Eastern Churches. Today both genuflecting and bowing are permitted in the Latin Rite. Both are an expression of our faith and of our reverence in the presence of the Almighty and of the Holy. At the very least, participation means that we bow or genuflect reverently. So much the better if our action reflects our interior sentiments of faith, of humility and of dependence on the Lord. When these external actions are done in this manner they manifest "soul." (See Discussion Starters, page 36.)

Our Surroundings Affect Our Participation

While the Eucharist is the mysterious mystical action of the Lord and our participation must be centered in our hearts, our surroundings have an effect on us when we are present at a Eucharist. Everything in a church is there to enhance our participation in the religious rites we celebrate. Every building which serves as a church says something about who God is and about those who come to worship.

I doubt that many of us very often hear what the building and its furnishings are telling us or that we reflect on how they affect our participation. We usually take for granted the shape, decorations and furnishings of the building. At most we may pay attention to the banners or decorations put up for special feast days. I know that the atmosphere of a small chapel puts me in a different mood than the one I experience in a school auditorium or in a large church.

When I visit different churches I like to reflect for a few moments on what thoughts and sentiments the building and its furnishings suggest to me about God, the community and participation. I find that the high vaulted ceilings in the large Gothic churches speak of the distance, the majesty and the power of God. The raised altar, the distance between it and the congregation suggest the distinction between the role of the ordained clergy and that of the nonordained People of God. The very atmosphere calls for wonder and awe. I usually pause in silent reverence. A church in the round with the altar in the middle or a fan-shaped building bring different images and feelings. They remind me that we are united, one people, all having a priestly role in a common activity. They call me to feel one with those present and to join in the singing and the prayers. The atmosphere of an auditorium or hall used for Mass speaks a very different language. It calls for less formality and more spontaneity. It offers more distractions, but it also speaks of finding the divine in the ordinary places we go each day.

We all have our preferences for the kind of building we think best helps us actively join in the worship of God. My pastor once stood in front of our modest, red-brick, German, nineteenth-century building and proudly said, "That is a church! The only way a church should be." I personally would have demolished it, but it had a message. It reminded me of the history, the faith, the generosity and the unity of the working people who built it. No building will please everyone nor have an obvious message like the new Los Angeles cathedral. When it was being designed, the architect, the liturgical consultant, the cardinal and his committee all were very conscious of the need of the people to be able to see and hear and so participate in the services. But they were also concerned about the feelings and the ideas the building with its furnishings would project to the people who looked at it. The design of every church has a message which colors the way we participate in the Eucharist. (See Discussion Starters, page 36.)

Over and above the design of the building, beautiful art, well-designed furniture and well-crafted liturgical items also foster participation. They are there for a purpose, which, when recognized, helps us focus our thoughts on what we are doing. Occasionally, it might be helpful to drop into a church and concentrate for a few minutes on one item, asking, "What does this suggest to me about what we do at the Eucharist?" For example, we could look intently at the crucifix and see what it suggests about what we do when we celebrate the liturgy. It might suggest to us the terrible price of sin and help us realize that through the Mass Jesus liberates us from our sins. It might suggest the astounding love the Lord has for us. In our mind's eye we might adjust that corpus and picture Jesus reaching down to embrace us and we reaching up in gratitude to embrace him. Or we may look intently at the altar and hear Christ calling us to come to his table to be fed. Focusing on the sanctuary light might help us realize that Christ is the light of the world and that he enlightens us at the Liturgy of the Word. The possibilities are countless for this type of remote preparation for the liturgy.

The building and its furnishings can enhance or hinder our sense of awe and wonder. The ceremonies, the homily, the singing can turn us on or off, but there is one other external element which is very important for our active, meaningful participation and that is the people in the pews with us. Is there a sense of unity, of being one in praising God, of doing this together? At times when I have sat in the pew I have felt this unity and it has helped me feel part of the celebration. Often I have felt alone and isolated and have retreated into my own prayers. I have felt this unity when I have celebrated or concelebrated in a parish where I knew some of the people and have felt that we were friends. I have experienced it when celebrating with the family at the bedside of a dying woman and, strangely enough, I have felt it in a cell block at a county jail.

We cannot do anything about the design of the church building except try to hear the message it offers. Usually we have little say about the church decorations or furnishings. There is one thing we can do about a community spirit. We can acknowledge people with a smile and a pleasant greeting as we approach the church door and as we leave the church. Often enough at first, people will not respond, but if enough of us try consistently to be friendly, others will catch the spirit. Then we will feel that we are with friends as we celebrate the Eucharist. (See Discussion Starters, page 36.)

Although our participation is affected by the church building, the furnishings and the people present, in the final analysis what is happening around us is of less importance than what is going on in our minds and hearts. We can receive the message and act on it even at the most spartan or desultory celebration if our eyes and ears are open to catch that which is beyond what is in front of them.

The Entrance Procession

Just as in any important celebration there is an introduction to the Eucharist which prepares us for what is to follow. These introductory rites before the first reading serve to unify us in spirit. They make us conscious of the fact that we are not praying alone, but that what we are doing, we are doing as one people gathered by Christ. They prepare us to listen to God's word and to celebrate the Eucharist.

Some sort of signal is given to call us to attention, to alert us to the beginning of the Eucharist. We rise. Some stand straight with hands folded. Others slouch with their hands at their sides or on the bench in front of them. Children wiggle and squirm. Often on Sundays a cantor will announce that the Eucharist is about to begin and ask the congregation to join in singing the opening song. We join in if we know the melody. Very often we simply listen to the choir. If there is no opening song someone will announce the page on which the Introductory Antiphon is to be found. Usually most of us read it aloud without understanding its meaning very well. In any case a signal is given to us to stand because the celebration has begun.

We do not know how leaders of small Christian communities in the first three or four centuries called the people to attention. Sometime after the fourth century, when Christianity became the official religion of the Roman Empire, the Eucharist was celebrated in large buildings. Some type of solemn beginning became necessary. The pope or bishop surrounded by the clergy would enter the assembly in a solemn procession while the choir and people sang a psalm. Today the Eucharist always begins with a procession. It may be a solemn one, begun at the rear of the church and moving up the center aisle, led by a cross-bearer flanked by candle bearers. The Gospel Book may be carried high in a cloud of incense and the readers and ministers of the Eucharist may precede the presiding priest. Or the entrance procession may be a simple walk-on, the celebrant and servers coming out of the sacristy onto the altar platform. Whether solemn or simple the obvious purpose is to get the presider to the altar with a certain amount of decorum and to focus the attention of the people on what is about to take place.

Standing at the beginning of an event also has a symbolic meaning. It is a sign of greeting and welcoming, as well as a sign of respect. Thus, at the beginning of the Mass we not only greet the celebrant and the other ministers, but we welcome Christ in the person of the priest. We welcome the Lord coming among us in his Word. We show our respect for the Lord as well as for all those who have gathered in his name. By this action we are also demonstrating our readiness to enter into the celebration and to do our part in it. With our physical eyes we see a congregation rising to its feet as the procession to the altar begins. With our ears we hear a Scripture verse or a song. With the eyes of faith we see the People of God entering into the presence of the Father to offer with Jesus his and our love and obedience. By our posture we are saying "let's get up and get going."

Processions or parades have a rich emotional symbolism. They recall important meaningful events. There are the parades on the Fourth of July as well as the Rose Parade at the beginning of the year. Each of these brings back memories. In a small town in Italy I once attended a procession from a chapel in the country to the village church. This procession had been held every year to give thanks for the end of a plague four hundred years ago. The entrance procession is a reminder that we are a pilgrim people making our way to our final home. We are a people who have no permanent home on this earth. We are constantly changing and moving on in our efforts to grow in the likeness of Christ.

It is true that we stand in one spot as the procession moves to the altar. We have a part in it either by singing the opening hymn or by reciting the Entrance Antiphon. These activities will indicate an active participation if our thoughts and feelings center on what we will be doing for the next hour or so. The words of the song or the Antiphon give us hints as to the direction of the Mass. They suggest an idea on which we may concentrate. They evoke a feeling which may color our prayers. They give us a clue about the aspect of the mystery which will be celebrated. As it were, they lead our hearts and minds into the presence of the Lord. We can try to put fervor into the words we say or sing or give ourselves over to the beauty, the joy or the majesty of the music. In some way, other than merely standing there, we need to become conscious that the mysterious mystical activity of God on our behalf is beginning.

The Entrance Antiphon

By opening our songbooks and being ready to sing along with the choir or cantor we acknowledge our unity with all the people in church and with believers all over the world. Singing the Entrance Song helps us pull our thoughts together. It makes it easier for us to rid ourselves of distractions. If the song has been chosen in view of the liturgical season or the feast which is being celebrated, it sets the tone for the entire celebration and fosters a feeling of unity with the Scripture readings and prayers of the Mass.

There is an old saying that he (or she) who sings prays twice. It is easy to see how this is so. Our thoughts are raised to God by the words as well as by the harmonious melody. Our voices convey feelings that often cannot find expression in the words. At least three factors work against our participation by singing. The first is our own voice. If we have a voice like that of a crow or if we cannot remember melodies, we usually are very uncomfortable trying to sing. However, someone has said that God has given us our voice and it is only right that he should have to listen to it. The second factor is the type of music selected. Classic church music appeals to some, while modern guitar music turns them off. Others enjoy modern music and are bored by the old hymns. Many parishes try to offer different types of music at different times. We have the freedom to choose the Mass with the type of music we enjoy. The third factor is the performance of the cantor, the choir and, especially, the musicians. An organ too loud can drown us in noise. A choir singing out of key can grate on our ears. A song leader can choose a pitch beyond our reach. No matter. We are not present for a concert. We are not present to perform or to be entertained. We are present to do our best with what we have in offering praise to God through song.

If there is no Entrance Song, we will recite a short Antiphon. Centuries ago this Antiphon was the verse the people sang between the verses of the psalm sung by the choir. It usually is a verse which embodies the spirit of the liturgical season or of the particular Mass which is being celebrated. Usually there is no time for us to ponder the verse and find the key idea it expresses. Perhaps if we would read over the prayers of the Mass in our missals before coming to church, we could hear what the Lord is saying to us through them when we recite them in church.

By this very first action, the liturgy summons us to come together and tells why we are coming together—Christ is here. It wordlessly summons us to participate and respond. The dialogue has begun. (See *Catechism*, #1156-1158, 1191.)

The Veneration of the Altar and the Greeting of the People

Usually while we are still singing or reciting the Opening Antiphon the priest will reach the altar, bow or genuflect, walk around it and kiss it. All these gestures are symbolic, and are made not merely in his own name but also in the name of all present.

The gestures the priest and the people make during the liturgy are not performed for their dramatic impact. They are meant to arouse or to express appropriate thoughts and feelings. Sometimes different gestures will reflect the same attitude because they arose in different cultures. Thus, standing, genuflecting and bowing all express humility and veneration. Bowing was the more customary sign of reverence in the culture of the ancient Middle East. Kneeling or genuflecting the more customary one in Western Europe. Both are used in the Latin Rite.

When the priest reaches the altar he bows and touches it with his lips, a symbolic action of respect and love for Christ. The altar is a symbol of Christ whose physical body was the altar on which the sacrifice that saved the world was offered once and for all. In the name of the people the priest is greeting and paying homage to the Lord. We can see this action as a sign of our realization that Christ is coming among us to feed us with his body and blood and to unite us with himself in the sacrifice he is continually offering to his Father. The fifth Preface for Easter puts it very clearly, "As he gave himself into our hands for our salvation he showed himself to be the priest, the altar and the lamb of sacrifice." For this reason and because it is the banquet table of the Lord, the altar is the center of the life of the Church.

Even such a simple thing as the chair on which the priest sits says something to us about what we are doing and how we are doing it. It may be ornate or very plain. It may be placed directly behind the altar or in front of it. It may be off to one side. No matter where it is placed it is a sign that each member of the Church contributes to the liturgy according to his or her function or role. The priest represents Christ as the head of the body and the chair is a symbol of his presiding over the assembly and of directing its prayer. (See *Catechism*, #1188, 1184.)

We join the celebrant in making the sign of the cross. By doing this we proclaim that we are members of the People of God who were marked with the cross when we joined the Church through Baptism and Confirmation. We express our faith in the Trinity and in the fact that we have been united to the one God through faith. We manifest our belief that salvation comes to us through the wood of the cross on which Jesus died.

It is not clear when the sign of the cross first came into use among Christians. At first the cross was such a sign of shame that it was not used by believers. The fish was a more common sign. The letters in the Greek word for fish (*ichthus*) are the first letters of the phrase, "Jesus Christ, God's Son, Savior." In time the cross became a sign of triumph rather than of shame. Saying it slowly with faith and gratitude endows our gesture with meaning. We make the sign of the cross so frequently that we can easily do it in a distracted and careless manner. Groups of people usually rattle through it at a rapid pace. At Mass we do not want to drag it out, but we can say it a bit more slowly and reflectively.

The celebrant greets us with extended arms and we respond. The greeting and extended arms of the presider as well as the response of the congregation is a welcoming embrace of all those present. It also expresses a deeper reality. The mutual embrace expressed by our reply, "and also with you," gathers in all those who have been baptized, living and dead. It is a sign of the entire Church gathered together under the headship of Christ. It expresses our unity with all the People of God in which no one is excluded because of economic status, race or cultural background, or lives which in some way are not in accord with the Gospel. (See Discussion Starters, page 36.)

We Acknowledge Our Need for God's Mercy

As part of our preparation to hear the word of God and to receive the body and blood of Christ we acknowledge that we belong to the throng of sinners whom Jesus welcomed, taught and fed. He surrounded himself with them. He forgave them even though they did not explicitly request forgiveness.

We are invited by the priest (or deacon) to be conscious of our sins. For many centuries there were no penitential prayers during the celebration of the Eucharist. They were introduced gradually in the early Middle Ages and often were said by the celebrant in the sacristy or during the procession. It was only in the sixteenth century that the *confiteor* became a fixed part of the Mass. It was said in Latin by the priest.

There are times when the Penitential Rite is omitted. For example, it is not said at a funeral Mass at which the priest meets and blesses the body of the deceased at the door of the church. Nor is it recited when the priest blesses and sprinkles the congregation with holy water at the beginning of Mass.

After this invitation by the presider or deacon there is supposed to be a short period of silence during which we are to bring to mind our sins. This silence usually is not long enough for us to do much of an examination of conscience. However, we can bring to mind one sin or one habit, such as egotistical pride, for which we are particularly sorry. In a few words we confess our sinfulness. Obviously each of us is asking forgiveness for our own personal sins. This request, whether in the long form of the "I confess," or in the short cry, "Lord, have mercy," the plea must come from our heart. It is a verbal expression of sincere repentance for what we have done by omission as well as by thought, word and deed.

We are also making a communal plea for forgiveness. As a Church we have not always put helping the poor high on our list of priorities. As a community we have often omitted to do what we can to correct injustice and to bring peace into the world. We have frequently neglected to proclaim that the Kingdom of God is at hand and to be convincing signs that it has indeed come. As a people we have failed in the mission entrusted to us by God.

The celebrant's prayer after the "I Confess" is not a form of absolution, as is that in the Sacrament of Reconciliation. Rather it is a plea for mercy with the unspoken realization that God always forgives. In fact, he has forgiven us before we ask. Theologians teach that participating in the eucharistic celebration with a contrite heart is one of the ordinary ways that venial sins are forgiven.

We Give Glory (Praise) to God

On Sundays, except during Advent and Lent, and on certain feast days we either sing or recite the Gloria. The introduction to *The Sacramentary* (the book which contains the instructions and prayers the priest needs to follow) says, "The Gloria is a very old and venerable hymn by which the Church, gathered in the Holy Spirit, glorifies and petitions God the Father and the Lamb" (see *The Sacramentary*, page 23, #31).

We do not know when the Gloria became part of the Mass. We find references to it in the sixth and seventh centuries. However, it could only be sung by a bishop. Priests were allowed to use it only at their ordination and on Easter. It was not until the eleventh century that they were allowed to use it regularly on specified days.

If the tune is familiar most of us join in the singing, but we still see a few standing silent. If it is recited, all too often we rush it. When I am with an unfamiliar group, sometimes I stop after a few words and ask the people to say it slowly and with meaning because it is an expression of praise to the Father, the Son and the Holy Spirit. We are recalling, thanking and acknowledging their loving actions on our behalf.

When the choir sings the entire Gloria we can surrender to the music and allow it to envelope us and bring to us the goodness and grandeur of God. If we are distracted by the music we might close our ears to all but the words and echo them with faith in our hearts.

The present position of the Gloria presents a bit of a problem if we are trying to flow with the feelings engendered by the prayers. We are asked to switch, without a pause, our attitude of repentance to one of praise. The penitential rite evokes a somber reflective mood. The Gloria calls for a joyful, exuberant mood praising Father and Son and asking for peace and the removal of our sins. Giving ourselves to the flow of the words and to the music in them can make the transition from one mood to the other natural and effortless. We have been forgiven. Now we express our joy. (See Discussion Starters, page 36.)

Let Us Pray

Another shift in mood occurs when the presider holds out his arms and says, "Let us pray." We have acknowledged our unworthiness. We have praised God. Now we are asking for a favor. Occasionally the priest will mention the intention for which we are being asked to pray. By his words he is calling us to be conscious that we are in the presence of God. His outstretched arms and raised hands are a gesture of peace, trust and supplication. They are a sign that we stand empty-handed before the Lord in great need of many things. They signify that he is gathering in all the needs and petitions which are in our hearts and is offering them to the Lord. Usually the celebrant will pause for a moment of silence. This pause gives us an opportunity to become conscious of our own requests that we wish to be included in the prayer he is about to offer. The purpose of this prayer is not to tell the Father what we need. God already knows that. Nor is it to convince the Father of our need. We cannot change God. The basic purpose is to remind ourselves that we are not in charge of our lives. We depend on God for all our needs.

The Opening Prayer as well as the Prayer Over the Gifts and the thanksgiving prayer at the end of the celebration are very terse and short. They all have the same structure. They seem to be very general. They certainly are not wordy. They say what they have to say in as few words as possible. Most people like this form of prayer because it is simple and direct. It meets the Lord's command that we do not babble on like pagans and think that it takes a lot of words to obtain God's favor (see Matthew 6:7). On Sundays there is an alternate longer, and usually more poetic, form of this prayer that the presider may use. Both the long and the short versions of the Opening Prayer, as well as the words of all the prayers said at Mass, have a secondary purpose. In a subtle way they are teaching us and forming our ideas and attitudes about our relationship to God. There is an ancient saying that what we pray expresses what we believe and what we believe shapes our prayer.

The basic structure of these prayers is very simple. The vast majority of them are addressed to God the Father. A few are addressed to Jesus and practically none are addressed to the Holy Spirit. Usually some quality of God, such as mercy or justice, is added to our call for the Lord's attention. This is followed by a request of a rather general nature. We ask for such things as forgiveness, faith, hope and love, and eternal life. The Prayer after Communion is usually a plea that the Eucharist will have an effect on our lives. The Opening Prayer, the Prayer Over the Gifts and the Prayer After Communion make their pleas in the name of Jesus. We recognize deep in our hearts that we have no right to be heard by Almighty God. We may even fear that God really does not listen to our puny words. But we are assured that we will get what we ask for, because Jesus promised, "whatever you ask the Father in my name he may give you" (John 15:16), and Saint Paul pledged that "we do not know how to pray as we ought, but the Spirit itself intercedes with inexpressible groanings" (Romans 8:26). The image that comes to my mind is one of confidently standing before the Father who cannot turn away anyone whom the Son and the Holy Spirit have made righteous and holy in his sight by their gifts of redemption and sanctification.

This "amen" at the end of the prayer is an affirmation of what the priest has recited in our name. It is a Hebrew word meaning "truly," "it is true," "so be it." It is a shout of praise and affirmation when uttered with understanding. In slang we might say, "right on," or "yeah, man!," or some other form of affirmation. It expresses our heartfelt agreement with the words which have just been said. For our "amen" to be more than a mechanical response at the end of a prayer we have to have been listening intently to what the celebrant has been praying. The words of the prayer have to have touched, not only our minds, but our hearts as well. If we have been distracted by watching what the other people are doing, if our minds have been wandering over the tasks that lay before us at home or work, if we have been critical of the way the ceremonies have been performed, our "amen" will have a hollow sound. We will not have a sense of thanksgiving and confidence that our prayer is being heard. We will not be ready to hear God's Word and to celebrate the Eucharist. On the other hand, if some word or phrase in the prayer has rung a bell for us and is an expression of our feeling of trust and gratitude, we will be ready to sit down quietly and allow the Scriptures to speak to us. A simple practice which can help us respond to the Opening Prayer with a hearty "amen" is to read it thoughtfully and prayerfully beforehand. Another simple practice that will help us appreciate the Opening Prayer, as well as the Prayer Over the Gifts and the Prayer after Communion, is to look at these three prayers in a Mass for the coming Sunday in a simple chart. To do so, make three columns. In the first column list the attributes of God that are mentioned. In the second list the things that are asked of God. In the third list the beliefs which are expressed in the prayers.

Take, for example, the Opening Prayer of the First Sunday in Ordinary Time. We address God as "Father of love." We ask three things—that he hear our prayers, that he help us know his will and that he give us the courage to do it with faith. We conclude by saying that we present these requests through our Lord Jesus Christ and the Holy Spirit—a very simple formula, but one that is most powerful. This prayer reminds us, or teaches us, that God is a God of love and all that implies. It tells us that our aim in life should be to do the will of God and it makes us conscious that we cannot do that will with our own power. Thus, it is a powerful teaching in very few words.

Copy the sample chart below and take the prayers from the Mass for the next two or three Sundays and identify these three steps. (Of course, there are slight variations on different days.) Then read one of the prayers reflectively and try to identify the faith ideas embodied in it.

A. Attribute of God	B. What we ask of God	C. Beliefs expressed

The "amen" to the Opening Prayer brings to a close the Introductory Rites. It is difficult to be conscious of the purpose of each of these elements of the Entrance Rite. However, a general sense of expectancy and of readiness to be a part of the action and an effort to respond with feeling and conviction will bring about that inner sense of belonging and of being a part of a great and glorious action.

DISCUSSION STARTERS

- *As the Eucharist begins, how do you try to tune in to what you and the others in the church are about to do?*

- *When you look at your church what does it seem to tell you about the nature of God?*

- *What do you like or miss in the decorations of your parish church?*
- *Complete the following sentence: I think the people in our parish are warm and friendly because they* _____ _____.

- *What do you usually do, think or feel during the Introductory Rites?*

- *Which kind of music most helps you be in touch with God?*

- *What do you think someone would read into the manner in which you make the sign of the cross?*

- *At the Penitential Rite I usually* _____.

- *During the Gloria I usually* _____.

PART THREE

The
Liturgy
of the
Word

First Reading, Responsorial Psalm, Second Reading, Alleluia, Gospel, Homily, Profession of Faith, General Intercessions

Speak Lord! Yours Are the Words of Life

As the Eucharist begins we stand shoulder to shoulder, not only with the people on either side of us, but also with many generations of believers. We are one with all those who have participated in the Eucharist for two thousand years. At first these ancestors of ours were few. They lived in a small area of the Near East and celebrated the Eucharist only on the Lord's Day. Today our brothers and sisters in faith live in every nation of the world and the Eucharist is celebrated daily. Except for the core action and the key words, the language and rituals of the celebration have changed greatly over the centuries and in various parts of the world.

For a few years after the events of Holy Week and Pentecost the small group of hearty souls who still professed belief in Jesus as the Christ continued to go to the temple to pray every day. Most likely in imitation of Jesus they continued to attend the synagogue. When they prayed they used the psalms and other forms of Jewish prayers. We still use the psalms as an integral part of our Catholic prayer life. Remnants of other Jewish prayers are still with us today in the liturgy. Jewish blessing prayers find an echo in the words the priest says over the bread and wine when they are brought to the altar. However, our blessing points to our gifts becoming the bread of life and the cup of salvation. Most importantly, the basic structure of the synagogue service survives today in the Liturgy of the Word.

The synagogue service consisted of two readings, one from the Law, that is, the first five books of the Old Testament, and one from the Prophets, or from one of the books we call the historical books. These were followed by a sermon or homily and by intercessory prayers. After the temple at Jerusalem was destroyed by the Romans in A.D. 70 the prescribed sacrifices ceased. The synagogue service continued to be, and still is, the Jewish form of communal worship. Then about the year A.D. 80 the Jewish Christians were no longer allowed to take part in synagogue services. Nevertheless, they continued in their house churches to have their own service of the Word in preparation for the celebration of the Eucharist. However, they had three readings. The first from the Law or the Prophets, the second from writings of the Apostles and the third from one of the Gospels. In time the Church cut the number of readings down to two, one from the Gospels and another from the other New Testament writings. Readings from the Old Testament were rare and were only used on certain special occasions, such as Good Friday.

The early practice was to read each book or letter in a continuous manner until the book or letter was finished. At each celebration the reader would begin reading where the previous reader had left off and read till the presider signaled a stop. Slight changes in this practice took place over the years. After a few centuries selections from the various books of Scripture, called pericopes, were assigned to be read on the same Sunday each year. No longer was an entire book of the Gospel or a complete letter read. Other minor changes, additions and reforms occurred at various times. In the reform of the liturgy mandated by the bishops at Vatican II the practice of having three readings on Sunday was reintroduced.

The Second Readings were chosen to give a "semicontinuous reading of the letters of Paul and James.... Only readings that are short and readily grasped by the people have been chosen" (from the Introduction to *The Lectionary*, #107). During

Advent and Lent it is rather easy to see a connection of the Second Reading with the Gospel and the First Reading. At other times they seem to have little connection with either of the other two readings.

On week days there are only two readings. There is a series I and a series II. The First Reading is either from the non-Gospel writings of the New Testament or from a book of the Old Testament. It is different in each series. In this way selections from all but the very short works of the prophets Abdiah and Zephaniah and from the Song of Songs are read during the two-year cycle. The Second Reading is from a Gospel, but it is the same in each series.

The latest revision of *The Lectionary*, that is, the book of readings, has been in preparation for some years and is not yet complete. At present, instead of a single book we have two books, one with the readings for Sunday and the other with the weekday readings. There is also a simplified lectionary to be used with children. The Introduction to *The Lectionary* gives a full explanation of how the various texts are arranged and of the norm used for choosing the texts we have.

Participation Is Not Only Hearing, But Also Listening

Our participation in the Liturgy of the Word seems to be very limited. We sit or stand and someone reads to us. Of course, we try to pay attention, but there are built-in distractions. These may be caused by the readings themselves. Often the biblical selections are short, out of context and seemingly unrelated. At times the names are strange and the references to the prophets or other incidents in the Hebrew Testament are difficult to grasp in a few short moments. Very often different ideas are striking our ears in too short a time or we can see no connection between the texts and our daily lives. The reader's style may also put us off. It is too dull or too dramatic, too loud or too soft. When these distractions occur we tend to close our ears to the words coming at us. What, then, can we ourselves do to receive "from God the word of his covenant through the faith that comes by hearing, and...respond to that word in faith, so that [we] may become more and more truly the people of the New Covenant"

(Introduction, *The Lectionary*, #45)?

To fully participate in the Liturgy of the Word it is not necessary to understand completely each of the selections. Our expectation of a helpful word and a positive attitude that we will hear the message from God is key to our meaningful participation. As we watch the reader approach the lectern there will be in the back of our minds some type of expectation. Do we anticipate being bored by readings we do not understand? Do we have a sense that what we will hear will not apply to life in this modern age? Is our attitude one of "Here we go again, dull readings, dull sermon"? Or is it a vibrant expectation that someplace in the readings will be that word, that message that will throw some light on our lives and fire up the love in our hearts? Do we have a vivid realization that through the words we hear God is talking to us trying to help us understand more fully his love for us and fanning our smoldering love for him into a brightly burning flame?

I know that my attitude is different on different days. I may be alert to all of the readings or I may concentrate my attention on one of them. I may expect to get a word from them or expect to hear nothing new. My attitude changes when I see who is coming to the ambo to read. But whatever my attitude is, it will determine how well I participate in the Liturgy of the Word. If it is negative, then I usually hear nothing pertinent to my life. I am in another world and the words will flow through my ears without even pausing. When my attitude is positive and I am anticipating a message, some word or sentence will usually give me pause and ring a bell for me. I will find some small nugget that is helpful and nourishing. I have found a comforting or enlightening word in passages poorly read or in a homily that has been poorly prepared or delivered.

What is the basis for a positive attitude which makes us open and receptive to the words we hear? Many factors enter into the formation of a positive attitude about anything. I can identify three which help me have a positive approach to listening to the Scriptures. First is the realization and acknowledgement that these readings are actually the Word of God, a loving letter from one who is concerned about me. Second is an element of hunger to hear what God will serve me today. I do not know what will be put before me but I know it will be spiritually nourishing. This hunger motivates me to pay close attention and to concentrate on what is being said. This hunger will not be satisfied if I am not willing to make a personal application of the readings to my own life and be open to changing my way of thinking. One person in our group said, "I have no problem applying the readings to the person in the pew with me, but often I do not see how they apply to me." Third is the belief that the readings are one of the means by which the saving and loving work of God is brought into my life here and now. Today God seldom appears to us in a pillar of fire, or as a cloud leading us to freedom, as he did the Israelites. But in his saving Word the Lord does come among us to guide and help us on our way to salvation and freedom.

Listen!

To participate in the Liturgy of the Word we need to listen. There are two forms of listening. One form is passive. We merely hear the sounds or the words. They strike our eardrums, but convey little of their message to our hearts. Just recall how often someone asked you what one of the readings was about and you could not recall it. You heard the words, but they went in one ear and out the other. There is also an active form of listening which is more than hearing. It is hearing with thoughtful attention. It involves understanding and absorbing in a personal way the meaning of the words which reach our ears.

Active listening to the Scripture readings requires some form of preparation. It can be as minimal as reading the three selections before Mass. It can be as thorough as spending time during the week reflecting on one or more of the readings and praying over them. Some people read one of the readings each day as the basis for their daily prayer. Still others read all three selections on the night before joining in the eucharistic celebration. There are groups who meet weekly to discuss the readings for the upcoming Sunday. This type of weekly group preparation is extremely valuable. We can think about and share what the readings mean to us. If we have a good facilitator we can learn about such things as the context of the passages, the meaning of various words and symbols, as well as the literary form the human writer used to pass on the inspired message. The selections from the Scriptures are not all the same type of writing. Some are stories; some are poems; others are prophecies, or visions; and a smaller amount are teachings and exhortations. Some form of preparatory reflection and prayer is necessary if we are to hear the saving message of God and be nourished by it.

Silence inside us and around us is also necessary if we are to hear God speaking to us and nourishing us. This inner silence needs to be combined with a clear proclamation made with feeling and conviction. Romano Guardini writes, "Faith can, of course, be kindled from the written text, the Gospel, the *glad tidings*, gains its full power only when it is heard.... The whole word is not the *printed*, but the *spoken*, in which alone truth stands free. Only words formed by the human voice have the delicacy and power which is necessary to stir the depths of emotion, the seat of the spirit, the full sensitiveness of the conscience.... The word of God is meant to be heard, and hearing requires silence" (*Meditations Before Mass*, pages 18, 19).

Sadly, it is not always possible to have the conditions which foster inner silence and make it possible for us to listen with attention. What we hear, and especially what penetrates our deepest heart, may be blocked by factors which are often beyond our control. Our minds might be on some pressing problem and the spoken word does not penetrate the block it poses to our attention. Our hearing may be impaired. We may not catch everything that is being read or we may have to strain so hard to catch the words that their message is missed. We may be a bit slow in grasping what is being read because we are one of those people who take in and process information more quickly and more easily by reading it than by hearing it. Our active hearing of the Word can easily be blocked by the reader who reads in a monotonous tone or is too dramatic. The reader may mispronounce words or have a very heavy accent. The church itself can cause us problems. There can be echoes or dead spots in the building which make it difficult to hear words clearly. There may be problems with the sound system. Children may be crying. We may be distracted by people coming in late. When any of these distractions occur, our tendency is to allow our minds to wander, to begin looking around the church and to turn off the reader.

What can we do if some of these obstacles to our hearing the message are present? We can concentrate on trying to catch the words, but this does not always help. Even though the ideal situation is for us to listen to the spoken word, at times following the readings in a missal or missalette helps us block out distractions and focus on the message. The ideal condition of a church with good acoustics and a faith-filled reader speaking clearly and distinctly with conviction seldom exists. When conditions for hearing the Word are less than perfect, having the printed words in hand helps us absorb the message better. Someone has said that we remember twice as much of what we both see and hear as we do of what we only see or hear. If we do use a missal or missalette we need to read the words slowly and thoughtfully, staying in sync with the reader so that what we hear penetrates through our eyes and ears to our hearts. (See Discussion Starters, page 58.)

The First Reading

Many times I have daydreamed about what it would have been like to have sat in a synagogue and listen to Jesus explain the Scriptures. It is hard for me to realize that when the reader opens *The Lectionary* to the First Reading from the Old Testament, I am hearing words that Jesus must have heard many times, words which he himself must have broken open for those present. Yet, as the reader's words flow through the church, I am being called to do what he and the other men in the synagogue did, namely recall and try to understand the events of the past and the hope for the future which they contain. In this reading we listen to the sacred writings of our Jewish ancestors. We learn about Solomon, David and the other kings of Israel. The words of the prophets calling the people to repentance strike our ears and the commonsense advice of wise men such as Sirach is laid out before us.

During the Liturgy of the Word there is a time to be silent and a time to talk, a time to listen and a time to respond. Now it is time to be silent and to listen. Many times the passages do not seem to have much relevance to our lives because we do not know anything about the situation in which they were uttered nor do we understand the manner in which God's love is being expressed. It is proclaimed in literary forms which are not too familiar to us. All the forty-six books of the Old Testament and the twenty-seven of the New Testament recount the care and concern God has for his chosen people, of whom we are a part. But the ancient writers used many different ways of communicating this theological message. For example, the stories such as those of the creation of the world and of the exodus are not meant to spell out in accurate detail what actually occurred. They are stories of the power of God and of his involvement in the lives of his people. The psalms speak of the same reality, but in a poetic form different than the ones we are accustomed to. They do not use rhyme and sentence structure the way we do. They compare, contrast, and develop a theme. Even when they repeat, the second line often develops the idea in the first. The words of the prophets, for the most part, had little to do with predicting the future. They were meant to encourage the people in bad times and correct them in good times. At times we may find in them foreshadowings of the mission and person of Jesus, but they always say something about our feelings and needs or about our relationship to God.

We are silent as the selection from the Old Testament is read, but are we listening? Often enough we are distracted or we cannot make much sense out of the reading. Our efforts at attentive listening are helped if beforehand we are given a few words situating the reading in history or indicating its purpose and message. This sentence usually looks ahead to the main point of the Gospel selection. What can we do if the reader does not give us this clue? As the reader announces the book from which the selection has been made, we might say something like this to ourselves, "I will listen closely for a word, a sentence and idea that will help me know or love or serve God better." By these words we alert ourselves to look for an enlightening thought, a comforting or a chastising word or an indication of how we might serve. Active listening is much easier if we have prepared ahead of time at home or before Mass. Reading the footnotes in the Bible, short simple commentaries or Sunday bulletin inserts will help us understand the context and the point of the words that we are hearing. Memories of a discussion we have participated in during the previous week or two about the relationship of the three readings help focus our ears, not only to hear, but to listen. It is not unusual for someone at our Wednesday group meeting to say, "That Old Testament reading or those words of Paul meant so much more to me Sunday after we had discussed it last week."

After we have listened there is a time to talk, a time to respond. At times our response to the reading will be silent and spontaneous. We will see how it applies to us and we will feel grateful for the insight. However, we are always called to voice our gratitude in the simple phrase, "Thanks be to God." Our sincerity in this response depends on how close we have paid attention to what was being read. Sometimes we have been intensely caught up in the reading. We have been like the alert fisherman standing hip-deep in a stream watching for that tiny ripple that signifies the presence of a fish. We have given all our attention to the event or the words being read in order to catch the food the Lord offers us this day. However, at other times we have relaxed, sat back and allowed the words to float past us without our being conscious that they are addressed to us. We have neglected to reach out, catch the message and draw it in. We have not listened. Our wandering thoughts have blocked the effort of the Holy Spirit to bring the message to life in our mind and heart. (See Discussion Starters, page 58.)

Responsorial Psalm

At the end of the First Reading we usually have a tiny island of silence. The reader pauses to give us a few moments to reflect on what we have heard. The reader or cantor then calls us to respond to the First Reading with a psalm which reflects its message. The reader or cantor recites or sings the verses of the psalm. After each verse we recite or sing a refrain which echoes a key idea from the reading. This form of back-and-forth singing or recitation is very ancient. One group sings or recites a verse. A second group sings or recites the next verse or repeats a refrain. At times we have trouble getting into this response. We cannot always follow the words of the singer, or we may not catch the response and so we will not know what to say or sing. In these cases it is useful to have a missalette at hand to help us. We cannot make a profound or prolonged meditation at this time, but some idea, some words or phrases will frequently surface and engage us.

One morning, as I sat listening to the story in the First Reading of David lusting after Bathsheba and murdering her husband to cover up his adultery, I was thinking what a conniving rascal he was. I wondered how God could have chosen a man so weak to rule the people in his name. As the reader finished speaking the thought struck me that I was in deep trouble if God only chose people of heroic virtue to carry out his plans. In ways different from David's I, too, am a conniver. In various other ways I, too, have put my desires and ambitions ahead of the will of the Lord. After only a slight pause, the reader began to read Psalm 51, and in so doing put the response on my lips, "Be merciful, O Lord, for we have sinned" (Year B, Friday of the third week of the year). It mattered not that I did not catch all the words of the psalm. I had heard enough to understand the message and the assurance of God's forgiveness to be able to respond with sincerity. (See Discussion Starters, page 58.)

The Second Reading

As we hear the lector announce the reading from one of the Letters (Epistles), or from the Acts of the Apostles, or from the Book of Revelation, we shift our concentration from the Old to the New Testament. We find it hard to listen, not to an entire letter, but to a section of a letter which was not addressed to us in the first place. It was sent to a particular church dealing with a particular situation a long time ago. A travelling preacher or apostle had told those first believers the story of Jesus and something of its meaning in God's plan for the human race. Like us, they had questions about what it meant. Like us, they misunderstood the implications for their daily lives of faith in Christ. Some disputed what Paul or Peter had taught. Others had fallen back into their old ways. Paul could not catch a 10:40 a.m.

plane and go in person to settle these problems. In fact, for a long time there was no way he could go, because he was in jail, so he wrote. John could not visit all the churches in Asia Minor, so he also wrote. Peter and James did the same. They wrote to specific people about specific subjects or problems. By the fact that these letters were exchanged between churches, we know that other people besides those to whom they were addressed saw the letters as applying to themselves. Centuries later we, too, see them as talking to us about our relationship to God, to Christ, to one another.

We face several problems in listening attentively to the readings during the Liturgy of the Word. We are not a group of new enthusiastic converts anxious to hear more about the meaning of Jesus and his message. We are not eagerly awaiting a reply to some question which has arisen in our community. We have heard these readings many times before, but most likely we have never read or heard a thorough explanation of the one now being read. As a result, we may not be sure about what the writer was getting at. We may not understand the references or the theological words. We may not like Paul because of his stance on this or that issue. In any case, it usually is impossible for us to listen to the words with anything like the enthusiasm the first Christians must have felt when someone opened a scroll and began to read aloud a letter from Paul to their community. Yet the letters are addressed to us. The Church has decided that these twenty-one letters contain God's authentic message for people of all time.

We face a problem. Usually we do not know the question or problem the writers were addressing. Even when it is clear in the reading we do not have the time to make the transfer to our own lives. All too often the wisdom, the light, the richness of faith which motivated the writers of the Letters goes right by us untapped.

It seems to me that some preparation beforehand will help attune our ears, not only to the obvious purpose of the selection, but also to some of its deeper implications in our lives. Taking a Scripture class on the Letters is a good long-range preparation, but one which many of us find difficult to do. Reading the passage beforehand at home is of some help, especially if we reflect on it and pray over it for a few minutes. Discussing the passage in a small group is, of course, a practical and useful way for most of us to be able to tap into the wisdom of these readings. I realize that I am repeating myself. The reason for doing so is simply that these discussions with a small group have been so helpful for me in understanding the readings and in preparing my homilies. We can also find enlightenment in the short explanations of the Second Readings which can be found in missals, in lectors' preparation books or in handouts about the Sunday liturgy. (See Discussion Starters, page 58.)

Alleluia

The reading ends. The cantor and the celebrant stand. We rise from our seats. We do not verbalize a response to the Second Reading, but one should be in our hearts in the few moments of silence before the joyful Alleluia is sung as a preparation to hearing the Gospel. We are, as it were, standing like the joyful crowd by the roadside as Jesus rode in triumph into Jerusalem. Christ is coming to us in a special way through the words of the Gospel. We, too, are enthusiastically crying out with joy, "Alleluia," which means, "Praise Yahweh...Glory to our God."

The Gospel

We stand as one body to listen attentively to the words of Jesus. He comes to talk to us as a group. In private reading, in prayer and meditation he speaks to us individually. But here, as we are gathered in his name, he speaks to us as a group, as he did to the crowd gathered on the hillside to hear his words. His words are meant to strengthen the bonds of unity we have, not only with him, but also with one another. We stand as a sign of respect and reverence, but also as a sign that we are ready to go out individually and as a group to bring the Good News to all the world.

In ages past and even today in many Eastern rites there is a solemn procession around the Church before the Gospel reading. The Gospel book is held high. Incense billows around it.

Today, at best, we have a very truncated procession. The altar servers carry candles and lead the celebrant or deacon who carries the Gospel Book from where it has rested in a place of honor in front of the altar to the ambo (reading stand). When the book has been placed on the stand the priest or deacon may incense it.

The use of incense at religious rites is an ancient practice. Several symbolic meanings are attached to it. Incense is used as a sign of honor and respect. One of the gifts of the Magi to the infant Jesus was incense. As we honor the Gospel Book we are paying honor not merely to printed words but to Christ himself who is present among us through this book. The incense is also a symbol of our prayers rising in sweet-smelling smoke toward heaven. It reminds us of the cloud by which God led his people to safety during the Exodus. The words of the Gospel are the means he uses today to lead us to life.

At other times the priest goes straight to the ambo. He silently prays, "Almighty God, cleanse my heart and my lips that I may worthily proclaim your gospel." As he does this, we can silently say a similar prayer asking God to open our ears to hear the words of Christ. We have a short familiar dialogue with the priest or deacon. He says, "The Lord be with you," and we reply, "And also with you." In the Old Testament whenever God said that he would be with someone it was an assurance that the project the person was undertaking would be successful. Mutually we are praying that this proclamation of the Gospel will bring us all closer to God and to one another. The priest or deacon says, "A reading from the holy gospel according to...." We respond, "Glory to you, Lord." The priest makes a small sign of the cross on the book, and then on his forehead, lips and breast as a plea that the Word will be in his mind, on his lips and in his heart. We can silently join this prayer of the priest as we make these three signs of the cross. We ask that the Word penetrate our minds and hearts so that it will be frequently on our lips. At the end of the reading he says, "The gospel of the Lord" to which we respond, "Praise to you, Lord Jesus Christ." The priest or deacon kisses the book as a sign of reverence and prays not only for himself but for us, "May the words of the gospel wipe away our sins." These very short exchanges, when said with faith and meaning, express our belief in the power of the Word which we have heard. The Gospel Book is not carried away from the ambo. It is left there as a sign that the Good News it contains is meant to be carried out in our hearts and on our lips. (See Discussion Starters, page 58.)

The Homily

At first glance, our involvement with the Homily seems to be mainly passive. Someone is speaking to us, reaching out to us. They talk. We listen. Usually it is only our bodies that are passive. Our minds are attentive and active. We hope to hear a word that touches our lives, a message that gives us insight into the situations we are facing. We would like a word of encouragement as we trudge along the path of daily routine. Frequently our desire is at least half fulfilled. We do get an insight. We do hear an encouraging word. We do see the way before us a little more clearly. Sometimes, however, we are disappointed.

The most frequent complaint about sermons or homilies is that they are boring, that they do not say something about *my* life. Each time we join in the celebration of the Eucharist we want the man up there to do all the work of bringing the Scriptures to life. In a perfect world every preacher would have a powerful message that goes right to our hearts and draws us into a deeper understanding of the Scriptures. The world is not perfect. Some homilists by nature are not dynamic preachers, nor are they able to prepare a soul-touching homily every time they approach the ambo. We who sit in the pews cannot do much about the quality of the sermons except to compliment the men who give a soul-touching homily and pray for those who do not.

What, then, do we do if the words we hear do not provide an insight into the reading and make it come to life for us? Some people shop around for a parish in which the priests on the whole are excellent speakers. Others, far too many others, simply stop attending the liturgy. Still others distract themselves in some way. One man says he sits in the pew outlining how he would present the message. Another counts all the mistakes in grammar and pronunciation the speaker makes. Others daydream, read the bulletin, look to see who is wearing what. One woman surreptitiously read a book during the sermon. These are all ways of coping with poor preaching when we place on the shoulders of the speaker all the responsibility for a message that will touch our minds or hearts.

I knew a grandmother who had a different approach. She listened for that one word or idea that spoke to her. She said, "I have never heard a sermon but that I got something out of it." Of course, she would have liked every homily to be soul-stirring, but she said that she had gotten something, maybe not much, from all the homilies or sermons she had heard. I suspect she was exaggerating. Instead of sitting in the pew silently complaining about the speaker, she opened her ears to the silent voice of the Holy Spirit and managed to hear a word of enlightenment or encouragement. Her attitude was that she had to make something out of what was said, even when the preacher had not done his part as well as he could. (See Discussion Starters, page 58.)

The Profession of Faith

On Sundays and feast days we make a Profession of Faith in response to the readings and the homily. It is a Profession of Faith by the community, that is, by the people and the priest together. Not all the readings nor all the homilies are such that they spontaneously call for a Profession of Faith. Nevertheless, whatever has been read and, it is to be hoped, whatever has been preached has cast light on the God in whom we believe. Therefore, once again we publicly proclaim the kind of God in whom we believe.

In the long history of the Church there have been many creeds or professions of faith. They were originally intended to be made at Baptism when a neophyte was publicly accepting a new way of life. The Apostles' Creed is the old baptismal formula of Rome. Later creeds were usually formulated in reaction to some heresy. They are meant to clarify the beliefs of the Church, which were under attack. For example, the Council of Nicea in A.D. 325 modified an existing creed to explicitly counteract the teaching of Arius, who denied that Christ was divine. The Council of Constantinople in A.D. 381 added the section on the Holy Spirit coming from both the Father and the Son in response to both Arius and Macedonius, who denied the perfect Godhead of the Holy Spirit.

A creed, not necessarily the Nicean Creed, was introduced into various liturgies at different times in history. It entered the Eastern liturgies much earlier than those of the West. For example, the Church at Antioch introduced a creed in A.D. 476, while the Church at Rome did not insert it into the liturgy until A.D. 1014. At that time the creed was already a regular part of the liturgy in the Holy Roman Empire (France and Germany). The emperor, Henry II, persuaded the pope to make it a regular part of the Roman liturgy. At different times it was sung or recited at a different place in the liturgy than it is now. For example, at one time it was said before the Preface, at another before Communion.

We are so familiar with the words of the creed that we frequently rattle them off without much feeling or thought. In fact, at times, the people in the pews seem to be having a race to see who can finish first. I want to call out, "Slow down! Think of what you are saying!" At the times when we have something to say, we need to utter the words with understanding and feeling because they are the foundation upon which we are trying to build our lives here and hereafter. We recite a statement which is not only a list of truths we intellectually accept, but is also a song of love. We are listing the qualities of the God we love as we would list the qualities of a human person whom we love. It is an expression of our placing our total trust in the God of whom we speak. For this reason we need to put feeling or "soul" into the words we recite. Our "soul-felt" utterance of these words then flows back into our hearts to strengthen our love and trust for the God who has done such marvelous things for us.

We may find that we cannot put much "soul" or vigor into the statements we make because we do not understand fully their meaning, or because we have questions about them. We may be adults with only a childish grasp of the meaning and implications of the statements of faith we make. In that case the very questioning or confusion is a call from the Holy Spirit to do what is necessary to get a better understanding of the truths we profess.

When we are reciting the creed in a group we cannot linger long over any of the statements. We can, however, make a quick mental check to see whether we do actually believe in what we are saying. I like to picture this process as being something like the quick check a person does of the cash receipt at a check-out counter in a supermarket to see whether all the prices are correct and whether something extra has been slipped in. If there is a discrepancy, the person stops and tries to get it straightened out. As the familiar phrases of the Creed roll off our tongue we silently ask ourselves, "Do I actually believe this?"

There are enough contrary voices from the media and the popular culture to raise doubts in the mind of a scholar or a saint. If we sense that what we actually believe does not resonate in our words, we can ignore the discrepancy and continue in the way we have been going, but our faith life weakens. Or we can check the item for a little more serious consideration because each of the statements has implications in the way we live. If after consideration we cannot understand how or why this is true, we can do as many do and drift away from the liturgy. We can also make an acceptance of it with the cry of the man whom Jesus asked whether he believed, "Lord, help my unbelief."

A quick example is the one word "God." Do we really believe that our God is different from all other gods? This idea is not too politically correct. We hear on all sides that "We all believe in the same God." This statement on the surface seems to be true. The vast majority of people profess a belief in a power beyond themselves and, in a sense, we can say that all people worship some god. That god may be power or money or pleasure. Even the atheist has a god which gives purpose to his or her life. It may only be a cause such as communism, or liberty, or the perfectibility of the human race, but it is something toward which he or she is striving. A generic belief in a god raises the much more fundamental question about what kind of god we worship. Merely using the word "god" to identify a higher power does not mean that we all mean the same thing. Certainly, the monotheism of the People of the Book is different from that of the pagan pantheisms. Among the People of the Book the God of the Christian is different from that of the Muslim or the Jew.

Only about a third of the human race profess a faith in a God who is three equal persons in one nature. The names we give these three persons are Father, Son and Spirit. Ours is a God who creates all things. Ours is a God who became human, did good things for people, died on a cross and rose from the dead. Ours is a God who is Spirit living in and with us. Ours is a God who judges the living and dead. In a very few short statements we express our essential understanding of what this God does for the human race. It is this God in whom we proclaim our faith, in whom we place our hope and whom we love. Each time we make the simple statement "We believe in one God" we are declaring something different from what the majority of human beings believe.

Just as our preparation of the Sunday readings enhances our appreciation of them, so, too, does our private or group reflection and discussion of the words of the creed make us aware of their deeper meaning and of their implications for our lives of faith. There are books we can read. More helpful seem to be adult learning groups which help us become clear about what we do think about God, Christ, and the Holy Spirit. They help us become aware of the importance of the words we have so often taken for granted. They open to us different perspectives than those we may have only learned in school. They help us see the relationship of the truths of our Profession of Faith to our daily work and to our daily lives. The cry, "I believe...," sounded with feeling and understanding, opens our hearts to the saving action of God that is about to begin after the General Intercessions, or Petitions. (See Discussion Starters, page 59.)

General Intercessions (Prayer of the Faithful)

By the time we have finished reciting the creed we notice that some of the small children are squirming in their places, leaning on the pew indicating they are bored. Their parents are distracted by these antics and are trying to have the children pay attention. The celebrant invites us to pray and a reader begins a list of petitions or requests. It's hard to tell how well people are listening to the requests and whether the response of "Lord, hear our prayer" comes from their hearts or is just a routine response to the request for prayer. At times the celebrant may ask for petitions from the pews. These can be interminably long or short and to the point. They can evoke a listless response or a heartfelt cry for help, depending on how deeply they touch the congregation.

From earliest times, Christians have presented petitions at the end of the Liturgy of the Word. The format is simple. The General Instruction of the Roman Missal in *The Sacramentary* says that "the intercessions may be made for the Church, for civil authorities, for those oppressed by various needs, for all mankind, and for the salvation of the world" (page 25, #45). These petitions are an official part of the prayers of the Church rising to the throne of God. They are short and to the point. However, if they are the same Sunday after Sunday they can easily evoke a rote mouthing of our cry to the Lord for help.

The degree to which we understand the purpose of these petitions will greatly influence the feeling we put into our request. We may not care much if someone is asking for help for a sick relative whom we do not know. We may feel very strongly if we are praying for an ailing pope or for the victims of a hurricane. This is a time when the local congregation is reaching out to pray for the needs of the members of the universal Church as well as for those of civil society. It is the time for us to be concerned with more than our own needs. It is a time to bring into the Eucharist all the world's problems and needs that cry to us from the TV and newspaper each day. It is a time for us to look out beyond the walls of the church and be conscious of the difficulties and suffering people out there are undergoing. It really is not a time for giving thanks for a favor received.

Even though our prayer is short it has a great depth of meaning. It is an acknowledgment of our total dependence on God. We realize that by ourselves we can do little or nothing about these situations. Yet at the same time it is an offer of whatever resources or abilities we have to be the tools God uses in the situation. Just because the problems are so big is no reason to push off all responsibility onto God's shoulders to make them right. In a real sense we are asking for enlightenment and guidance about what we, as a community and as individuals, can do about these situations. A better way of expressing this might be to say that the cry, "Lord hear our prayer" is a request for God to open our eyes and ears to cooperating with the Lord in helping those in need. God usually works through human beings to right wrongs and to solve problems. Our offer to help sounds very unrealistic. But if we think about it, often there is something we can do. We know that we cannot do anything about the millions of children who go to bed hungry every night, but we can feed one more child. We know that we do not have much voice in the affairs of the government or the Church, but we can let our voice be heard in one way or another. We cannot do much about the priest shortage, but we can encourage one young man to consider the priesthood. We cannot cure a child with cancer but we may be able to offer a supporting arm to its mother. The very least we can do is pray frequently for guidance and strength to do what we might be able to do. In other words, as the priest says the prayer ending the General Intercessions, we do not wash our hands of all the problems of the people outside the walls of our church. Instead our attitude is that of the prophet Isaiah who cried out, "Here I am...send me!" (Isaiah 6:8). We affirm our resolution with a fervent "Amen" when the celebrant ends the General Intercessions with a short, often spontaneous, plea that our requests be granted because we are asking in the name of Jesus, our Lord. (See Discussion Starters, page 59.)

DISCUSSION STARTERS

- *What is most distracting to you during the readings?*

- *Complete the following sentence: I do or do not follow the readings in the missalette because* _____.

- *Why do you think you sometimes have trouble understanding the First Reading?*

- *How do you usually respond during the Responsorial Psalm?*

- *What are the reasons you feel that you do or do not understand the Second Reading?*

- *What do you usually do during the reading of the Gospel?*

- *What are the reasons that you usually do or do not get something out of the Homily?*

- *When questions about one of the articles of the Creed arise in your mind what do you usually do about this?*

- *What are your feelings about the General Intercessions?*

PART FOUR

*Liturgy
of the
Eucharist*

The Offertory,
Preparation of the Altar
and the Gifts, Preface,
Eucharistic Prayer,
Communion Rite,
Concluding Rite

Let Us Give Thanks to the Lord Our God

The homilist steps away from the ambo and goes to his chair. A period has been put to the Liturgy of the Word. We sit. The ushers take up the collection. We have a few minutes for reflection. We may feel uneasy. We are not used to being quiet and reflective, especially during the Eucharist. We have reached a transition point. We have heard God's written word proclaimed and explained. We are waiting for the Liturgy of the Eucharist to begin. If the choir is singing we may relax and listen to the music. We may ponder what we have heard in the Scripture readings. We may mull over what we have heard in the homily. We may pray quietly within ourselves. We may reflect on the mysterious action of God in which we will share during the Liturgy of the Eucharist. Whatever we do, we are preparing ourselves to participate in the core action of the Mass, the Liturgy of the Eucharist.

We will drop our donation into the collection basket, make a few responses, join in a song or two. We will sit while the Table of the Lord is being set. We will kneel (or for a good reason, stand) during the Eucharistic Prayer itself. The seeming inactivity is a challenge. Will we merely watch in a detached manner, daydream, be bored or will we plunge wholeheartedly into the mystery? Will we welcome the real presence of Jesus and join him in offering thanks to the Father? This kind of participation is a big order. It calls for a radical kind of faith which truly sees that which cannot be seen, which hears that which is inaudible and which believes that which seems unbelievable.

It is impossible to give a simple formula which will help us "get something more out of the Mass." It seems to me that there are one or two rather simple things which will help bring the meaning of the celebration into sharper focus for us. Of course, prayer, reflection, meditation are the primary resources we have to delve into the mystery of the Eucharist. In addition to these we need a mind-set, a way of understanding and appreciating what is going on, a way that makes us conscious of the fact that we are involved through symbols and signs with a mysterious mystical reality that is at the heart of our very own lives. This action holds the secret to the meaning of life for us and to our ultimate destiny. Digging into the rich symbolism of the prayers, the ceremonies and even the objects used at Mass can help us grasp the reality which is occurring before our eyes and of which we are a part. We need to look beyond a beautiful setting, or soul-stirring music or an inspiring homily to Christ becoming personally and really present among us, drawing us into his love. This understanding is the basis of a eucharistic spirit, a spirit of love and gratitude. This spirit, not the desire to be entertained or educated, puts eagerness into our steps when we realize that it is time for daily or weekly Mass. It focuses our attention while the priest is praying in our name. It brings the peace and joy of Christ into our daily lives. Of course, the clarity and intensity of this realization will vary from week to week, but it will be the basic, powerful guiding motive for our being present and taking part in the celebration of the liturgy.

We are being put in touch with the indescribable beauty, the overwhelming power and the immeasurable love of the invisible but present God. It is difficult, if not impossible, to describe the experience of being caught up into the mystery which is occurring before our eyes. However, we can put aside thoughts

64

which stray to our everyday concerns and to expectations which can only be met by what someone else does and concentrate on what the Holy Spirit is doing for us.

This interior type of participation of our hearts and our minds is possible only when faith guides our thoughts and feelings. Faith is more than accepting ideas because God has revealed them. It is acceptance enshrouded in mutual love. When we are in love with a person we want to be with that person. We want to know all we can about that person. We want to share our lives with that person. We realize that we are important to that person. Our faith also tells us that God is in love with us and that we are important to God. This love is so great that God shares his life with us and welcomes our sharing our joys and sorrows, our successes and failures with him. It is this belief that makes the Mass alive and exciting. (See Discussion Starters, page 85.)

The Offertory Collection

Ushers quietly and quickly begin taking up the collection. We fish in our pockets or in our purses for the Sunday envelope or for a bill to drop into the collection basket. The children finally have something to do. They stand up, reach out and with a flourish drop coins into the basket. A very small part of the money collected will be used to buy the bread and wine which will be blessed and used for the Eucharist. The greatest part of it will be used for the works of the parish. It will build and maintain the buildings, support the clergy and care for the needy. It is our gift to the community.

From the very early days of the Church the people have brought gifts to the Eucharist for this same purpose. When the Eucharist was joined to a common meal the people would bring food which was supposed to be shared by all. Some bread and wine was set aside for the Eucharist. After the Eucharist was separated from the common meal the custom continued. People would bring small loaves of bread wrapped in a white cloth and small jars of wine, along with other things such as oil, fruit, wool and money. These would be brought in procession to be handed to the deacons who would set aside enough bread and wine for the Eucharist. The rest would be used for the needs of the poor and the support of the clergy. This Offertory Procession took many forms over the intervening centuries. For the most part it died out centuries ago, until it was revived after Vatican Council II in the form we now have it.

Today we usually see a small procession of not more than a half dozen people bring the gifts of bread and wine to the priest or deacon. After the altar has been prepared by the altar servers, who place the linen corporal, the purificator, the chalice and the missal there, several people will rise from their seats, pick up the bread and wine, carry them to the foot of the altar and present them to the priest or deacon. At times an usher will join the procession carrying the collection which will be placed near the altar. Many times the procession is even shorter than that. The altar servers bring the bread and wine from a side table and place them on the altar. Most often we do not pay much attention to this procession. Yet it is a visible sign that all present are participating in this celebration. Symbolically we are acknowledging that we are responsible members of the Catholic community and we are providing the materials to be used by the priest to bring Christ among us in the eucharistic species. (See Discussion Starters, page 85.)

Preparation of the Gifts

As we sit and watch the gifts being prepared on the altar we usually do not get much of a feeling that we are being invited to take our place at a banquet. It was easier for the first Christians to visualize Christ coming among them during a banquet. They were sitting at a table on which was their daily bread. Today the banquet is stylized. It is a set ritual. It serves to prepare the bread and wine in a dignified way. It also recalls the action of Jesus, who sent two of his disciples, Peter and John, to the house of a friend to prepare the table for his last supper with them. This preparation involved seeing that the room was ready and that food was present, especially bread and wine (see Luke 22:7-13). Our preparation does not look much like that made by Peter and John. Nevertheless, that is what is occurring.

In early Medieval times priests were uncomfortable with silence. They felt that every liturgical action needed to be accompanied by prayers. As they received the bread and wine that were being brought to the altar table they quietly said a prayer over each of them. Today, the celebrant is supposed to say these prayers quietly if the people are singing. If there is no singing the prayers are to be said in an audible voice.

The short prayers said over the bread and the wine set them aside from ordinary use and designate them for a sacred purpose. These prayers are very similar to Jewish meal prayers. They remind us that the bread and wine we have on the table are the result both of the action of God and of human beings. God gives the sun, the rain and the grain and the grapes. Human beings make the wheat into bread and the grapes into wine. In response to the presider's prayers we praise and thank God with a fervent, "Blessed be God for ever."

Before the celebrant prays over the wine he pours a few drops of water into it. The origin of this practice is not clear. Perhaps it arose from the custom of cutting wine with water. However the symbolism of this tiny action is profound. It expresses two great truths. The first is that Christ who is divine became human. The second is the reason he did so. It was that we who are human may share in his divinity—"...may we come to share in the divinity of Christ who humbled himself to share in our humanity." If we allow these two truths to percolate in our minds during the few minutes it takes the celebrant to prepare the gifts, gratitude, hope and trust will flood our hearts.

The celebrant washes his hands. In days gone by, when the gifts were placed into the hands of the celebrant he would wash his hands before proceeding to the Eucharistic Prayer itself. Today it is a sign of his desire for inward purification. As we watch the water being poured over his hands, we can also silently ask that God will take away our iniquity and wash away our sins. Finally, we are asked to pray that the sacrifice that will be offered may be acceptable to God. As a community we pray that our sacrifice will result in glory to God, to our good and to the good of all the Church. The priest then says a short prayer, usually asking once again that God will accept the gifts we have to offer. To this we answer with a resounding "Amen." We certainly do hope that what we are doing is pleasing to God.

During the Preparation of the Gifts it is easy for our minds to wander. We are sitting and the priest may be praying in a low voice. The altar servers may distract us because they are not as reverent as we would like them to be. The hymn being sung may direct our attention not to what is going on at the altar but to some other pious reality. What can we do to stay focused on the sacred action happening before our eyes? The first and most obvious way is to listen carefully to the short prayers being said and echo them in our hearts. If we do not hear them clearly we can always follow them in a missalette. We might concentrate on just one of them at a time until it becomes part of us. For example, the prayer said at the mixing of the water and wine sounds strange to our ears. We are used to speaking of ourselves as sons and daughters of God, as brothers and sisters of Jesus, as temples of the Holy Spirit, but to share in the divinity of Christ sounds like another matter. We can well reflect on that simple prayer week after week in the few moments of silence we have at this time. Mulling over the meaning of the prayers and of the ritual helps us become conscious of the fantastic, improbable, mind-boggling purpose of the Lord in giving us the Eucharist. (See Discussion Starters, page 85.)

The Preface

After we have put our Amen to the Prayer Over the Gifts we stand. We have a short dialogue with the priest. These three short exchanges raise the question about what has been going on in our minds and hearts so far, and especially about what will be stirring in them in the next few minutes. The celebrant begins by calling for our attention because something important is about to occur: "The Lord be with you." He has said this several other times during the Mass. Our response, "And also with you," tells him that we are with him at this point and that we are focusing on what we are about to do. Before beginning the crucial part of the Eucharist, he tells us what is expected of us during the coming moments. We are to lift up our hearts, that is, we are to give full and complete attention to what he is about to do. We tell him that we will do just that and we imply that we have been doing that all along. "We lift them up to the Lord." (Time out here. Is our response truthful and authentic? Where have our hearts been? Bored, focused on what other people have or have not been doing, centered on God reaching out to us?) Then the celebrant urges us to give thanks to the Lord our God, and we agree, "It is right to give him thanks and praise." The priest then tells the Lord that we always and everywhere give him thanks through Jesus Christ our Lord and he mentions one or two reasons for our doing this. When he is finished we joyfully cry out or sing the Holy, Holy, Holy, which is our praise to the Lord God and to him who comes in the name of the Lord.

Having our minds and hearts in the responses we have made and our full attention focused on the reasons we have for praising the Lord God is participation at the highest level of our being. Of course, we have to struggle against the tendency to respond automatically without much thought because we have heard the words so many times before. But the great variety of Prefaces is the antidote to a lifeless repetition that makes us insensitive to the fundamental gratitude we are trying to express. There are now more than a hundred Prefaces, each highlighting some particular aspect of the goodness of God. It is helpful, by ourselves or with a group, to read the Preface for the coming Sunday and discuss the reason it gives for gratitude and whether this particular reason means much to us. (See Discussion Starters, page 85.)

Eucharistic Prayer

We come to the core moment of the Mass. According to the practice of our parish, we kneel or stand during the Eucharistic Prayer. The Liturgy of the Eucharist involves a great leap of faith. What we see and hear is not what we get. We see bread and wine and we get the real presence of Jesus, body and blood, soul and divinity, among us. We hear an account of Jesus' actions and words at the Last Supper and we get Jesus' sacrifice, which brings salvation to the world. What we see and hear are just external signs of what is occurring in a hidden manner through these signs.

At this point in the celebration we are called to be conscious of, to be open to, to trust in the invisible action of the Holy Spirit drawing us into loving union with the Trinity. In spite of what our eyes and ears tell us, we know that a great spiritual drama is taking place. We are being drawn into the greatest act of love that God has ever shown the human race—the life, sufferings, death, resurrection and ascension of Jesus the Christ, his sending of the Holy Spirit and anticipation of his final coming. By faith we realize that through what we see and hear at the altar we are being invited to take part in this stupendous, generous, loving act of God. At best, what we see and hear can only give us an inkling of what is actually happening.

We have very little to say or do at this time. Perhaps this is the time to reflect on why we actually come to Mass Sunday after Sunday, or day after day. Of course we have come to pray, but if that is all there is to the service we could pray alone. We could have stayed in bed and prayed at a later time. Of course, we have come to be inspired by song and word, but we could have easily read more uplifting words and heard more inspiring music alone or with a few friends. Why then have we come?

The answer to our question is not a clear-cut, easily understood flow of words. We cannot reduce to human language what is occurring before our eyes. We need to suspend our ordinary, pragmatic, practical understanding of words and actions and open ourselves to a different kind of comprehension which comes when feelings, memories, dreams and intuitions flood over us and change the way we see, hear and think. The words and the actions seem to be crying out to us, "Delve beneath us. Put aside the way you understand us every day. Enter into the world of the divine mystery which is more real than reality itself. The reality which you see and hear is more unlike what is occurring than like it. You are being caught up into the realm of the divine, of God's mysterious love and action in your life. Sing, 'Alleluia!'"

Questions such as "how? when? why?" about how this is achieved can never be adequately answered. It is only by faith that we can know and appreciate that we have been called to be present and to take part in this wondrous action. (See Discussion Starters, page 85.)

We use two ordinary words, "celebration" and "memorial," to express what occurs at this time. These two words have a much richer meaning than we usually give them. A celebration suggests honoring somebody or something by solemn ceremonies. Frequently it implies an enjoyable event such as a dinner. We are doing this. A memorial is something done in memory of someone or some event which keeps alive the memory of that person or event. We are doing this. But we are doing much more. Certainly, the Eucharist is solemn and it keeps alive the memory of the life, death, resurrection and ascension of Jesus and holds out the promise that he will come again and we will share eternal life with him. This action looks beyond time and place. It looks to the past. It recalls all that Jesus did to liberate us from the bondage of sin. It is anchored in the present because that one definitive sacrifice of Jesus is made present and offered in an unbloody manner in our midst. It holds out hope for the future when we who have profited by this one death will gather for the eternal heavenly banquet. But the Eucharist is a unique kind of celebration. It not only keeps alive Christ's memory. It also makes the Lord and his power present among us here and now, twenty centuries later. Jesus died once, and he cannot die again. He offered one sacrifice and we can offer no other. Yet, in a mysterious way he comes among us really and personally. We are privileged to join with him in offering his sacrifice on the cross, which is made present on our altar. We have nothing to which we can compare this type of memorial, this making present of an action which occurred twenty centuries ago. Faith alone tells us that it is so.

Another unique aspect of this celebration is that this memorial, this commemoration, is the prayer and action of the risen living Christ acting through a human agent, the priest. It is the risen Christ now united with his Church who offers for us and with us worship and praise to the Father. However, without the prayer of the designated human agent there is no eucharistic liturgy. Believers may gather in the name of Jesus. There may be a service of prayer and Scripture reading. There may even be a sharing of bread and wine. But without the priest, not only acting in the name of Jesus, but being, as it were, the very mouthpiece of Jesus praying with and for his friends, there is no Eucharist. If the priest says a hurried form of this prayer over a tiny bit of bread and a sip of wine, the mystery of the life, death and resurrection of Jesus becomes present to bring life and hope to those participating. There are stories of priests in Nazi concentration camps celebrating a hurried, silent Mass with a morsel of bread and a small amount of smuggled wine. Christ was there really, truly and substantially to strengthen and feed those prisoners with his body and blood. (See Discussion Starters, page 86.)

Over the centuries the Church in various parts of the world has celebrated the banquet and the sacrifice of the Lord in different ways. They all have centered on the words and actions of Jesus at the Last Supper. It is enlightening to attend the liturgy in an Eastern Catholic Church, which celebrates the Eucharist according to one of the Eastern Rites, such as the Byzantine or Melkite rite. We can usually easily identify the various parts of the liturgy. We all are involved in the same great mystery, but each of us is doing it according to our tradition and customs.

We of the Latin Rite have used the Roman Canon for sixteen centuries with only a few slight changes over time. (The word "canon" comes from the Greek word meaning "rule.") Its basic structure was set by Pope Damasus at the end of the fourth century. At that time he also made Latin instead of Greek the principal liturgical language of the West. Since the reform of the liturgy mandated by Vatican Council II, we have been given the option of using various other Eucharistic Prayers. Besides the first Eucharistic Prayer, which is the Roman Canon, there are at present twelve other Eucharistic Prayers that may be used on special occasions. They all are solemn prayers calling for a spirit of adoration, awe and wonder. They all are prayers of thanksgiving and sanctification. With each of them we "join Christ in acknowledging the works of God and in offering sacrifice" (Introduction, *The Sacramentary*, pages 25-26).

The Eucharistic Prayer is introduced by a Preface of which there are at least one hundred designed for different liturgical seasons or for special occasions. The Preface and the Eucharistic Prayer give thanks to God for his goodness manifested in so many different ways. They deserve to be reflected upon line by line to allow the realization of how good and powerful God is.

The various Eucharistic Prayers used in our Latin Rite all have the same eight parts:

1) Thanksgiving that is expressed very clearly in the Prefaces. Each emphasizes some particular reason we have for thanking God.

2) An acclamation of praise in which we join with the angels and saints to sing or say, "Holy, Holy, Holy," and so on.

3) An invocation (in Greek, *Epiclesis*) recited before or after the words of institution calling upon the Holy Spirit to come down upon the sacred bread and wine and dwell within it and in the hearts of the faithful.

4) The telling of the words and actions of Christ at the Last Supper.

5) A short prayer fulfilling the Lord's command to remember what he did, especially his Passion, Resurrection and Ascension.

6) An offering of the Sacrifice of Christ to the Father in the Holy Spirit.

7) Intercessions for all the members of the Church, both living and dead, who share in the redemption and salvation won by Christ.

8) A final exclamation of praise to the Trinity, to which the people make an assent of belief by saying or singing, "Amen."

The second Eucharistic Prayer traces its ancestry back even further than the first Eucharistic Prayer. Its basic outline and sentiments are found in the writings of Saint Hippolytus at the beginning of the third century. It is the shortest of the Eucharistic Prayers and expresses all the essentials. The Sanctus and one or two other elements were added later on. It was only restored for use in the Latin Rite in 1969, but it has been in constant use in the Ethiopian Church from its beginnings.

The third Eucharistic Prayer has no Preface of its own. It is to be used with the variable Prefaces. It is a modern creation which incorporates ideas such as the Church being the People of God and the unity of all believers. It unites these ideas with traditional biblical themes used in the ancient liturgies of France and Spain. It is at once contemporary and traditional.

The fourth Eucharistic Prayer moves from creation to our final glory in the Kingdom of God. It is modeled after some of the Eastern liturgies associated with Saint Basil (c.330-379). Sections of it may go back as far as the fourth century.

The children's Eucharistic Prayers have been simplified to make them more comprehensible to little ones and to give children more opportunity to participate vocally.

The Eucharistic Prayers for Masses of reconciliation emphasize the greatness of God's love and forgiveness, especially through the life and activity of his Son, Jesus Christ. (See Discussion Starters, page 86.)

The Consecration

The Eucharistic Prayers we hear on Sundays are built around the words Jesus spoke at the Last Supper, "This is my body.... This is my blood.... Do this in memory of me." The Church has always understood them literally and has reaffirmed this understanding many times in history. The present *Catechism of the Catholic Church* reasserts the definitive teaching of the Council of Trent given some four hundred and fifty years ago, "In the most blessed sacrament of the Eucharist, the body and blood together with the soul and divinity, of our Lord Jesus Christ and therefore, the whole Christ is truly, really, and substantially contained" (*Catechism*, #1211). The bishops at that time, those at the Second Vatican Council, and the present pope were not expressing some out-of-date belief. They were merely reiterating the age-old belief of the Catholic Church.

Some people have problems believing in the real presence because they understand this teaching as expressing a physical presence of Christ. We need but look at the host and the consecrated wine to see that they are not physically Christ. On the other hand, the Eucharist is not merely a sign of his presence, nor a mere symbolic presence. Through the power of the Holy Spirit, in a way we do not understand, the whole Christ is truly, really and substantially present. The challenge to believe in this presence is asking for more than an assent in our heads that Christ is here in a mysterious way different from any other way he is present among his people. It is more than a call to praise, thank and adore him. It goes much deeper than that. Each time we see the sacred host and the sacred cup elevated we are being called to participate in this mysterious mystical action by the Holy Spirit by making it our own and by living out the values Christ taught and manifested. It is a call not merely to participate in this Mass, but to unite our total selves with the living and real Christ in and with his body, the Church.

Every time I elevate or see elevated the sacred species I hear questions asked of me and of those present: "Do you believe in the real, substantial presence of Christ under the appearances of bread and wine? Do you believe that the same Jesus Christ who walked the earth two thousand years ago is on this altar, resurrected and alive but changed?"

Obviously Christ is not present in the form he had when he preached and taught in Galilee. The Gospel writers tell us that after the Resurrection he was different, very different than they had previously known him. He appeared in a room with locked doors. Two of his disciples did not recognize him, though they spent an afternoon walking and talking with him. Finally, he simply vanished from the sight of his disciples after he had commissioned the eleven to go and preach to the whole world. Those first disciples recognized that the manner in which Jesus the Christ was present to them was unique. The manner in which he is present to us is even more unique. The bread and wine are not merely signs or symbols of Christ's presence. The whole Christ is really, truly and substantially present. This presence can only be recognized by faith. Our eyes cannot see him. Our hands cannot touch him. Our ears cannot hear him. Only faith can recognize and accept his presence.

The challenge I hear is not only to believe with my whole being that Christ is really and truly present, but also to offer him adoration, to become more firmly united in love to him and to all the members of his body, the Church, and to try to live by the values he taught. All of these sentiments are summarized in a fervent silent phrase, "My Lord and my God."

After the consecration of the wine we say or sing one of the four memorial acclamations. Each expresses a different aspect of what we believe is occurring in our midst. They are short statements that bring to memory what Christ has done for us. They are acclamations because they are intended to proclaim loudly and fervently our belief that Christ is here and now doing the same for us and that he will continue to do so until he comes again. Our "Amen" at the end of the Eucharistic Prayer is our affirmation that we believe in and approve of what the celebrant has been praying. Our "Amen" is our robust approval of what Christ is doing in our midst. It means something like a hearty, "So be it!" At times we sing it and repeat it three or more times to emphasize how deeply we feel about it.

Whether we kneel, stand or sit, whether we have things to say or do during the Eucharistic Prayer is much less important than what is occurring in our minds and hearts. Our sense of belonging, of being a part of what is occurring, of finding meaning in what we are doing depends on what is going on inside us. If our minds are distracted, thinking about what we have to do in the coming week, if our hearts are apathetic and cold and if a lack of understanding or if disbelief colors our thinking we will find little or no sense in what is happening before us. Then the look on our face, the positioning of our body, the expression in our voice may tell those around us that we are bored, indifferent or concerned about other things.

On the other hand, if we have some understanding of the fact that by the power of the Holy Spirit the bread and wine become the body and blood of Christ and that we, as a community of believers, are gathered around the table of the Lord, we will unite ourselves with the action of the Mass. This inner belief will show itself externally in the manner in which we proclaim our faith at the memorial acclamation and at the great Amen which ends the Eucharistic Prayer. The feelings we put into the tone of our voices as we say these short exclamations usually is an indication of how much we feel that we have been involved in the ceremony.

It is not easy to put into words the thoughts and ideas, as well as the memories, hopes and sentiments which lift us out of the present and place us in union with Christ at the throne of God. Each of us will be moved by different ideas and different sentiments. Our imagination needs to be at work, not to create an illusory picture of what the Mass is about, but to put us in touch with the reality of Christ's presence so inadequately expressed in the prayers. Our images and our faith in the Eucharist need to be guided by the wisdom and understanding of the Church.

People who attend Mass regularly usually realize that in some way Jesus, alive and with the power of God, comes to them concealed under the appearances of bread and wine. They want to be more closely united with him and to his body, the Church. Usually they will make an interior act of faith in the real presence when the sacred host is elevated at the time of the consecration. Most of them will receive Communion. However, their interior participation may be handicapped because they do not have a very clear idea of what the liturgy is and its role in their spiritual life. Many are still guided by the simple explanations of the Mass found in instruction books for children. These usually are not dynamic and meaningful enough to sustain the faith and practice of adults, especially of young adults. This fact makes it obvious that as we grow up our knowledge and understanding of the Eucharist need to expand and become more profound. Each of us does not have to become a theologian, but we do need an adult understanding of the Mass. There are books and talks available to fit all levels of people's needs. A great help in fostering an adult appreciation of the Eucharist are the four or five pages (ten sections) of the Constitution on the Sacred Liturgy issued by the bishops at Vatican II and in the sections #1066 to #1419 in the *Catechism*.

A simple way to foster this sense of interior participation is to read slowly and meditatively one of the Eucharistic Prayers before going to church. The words of these prayers will evoke images and sentiments which will come to mind later when we hear them from the altar. They will evoke expressions of faith, as well as sentiments of gratitude, awe, wonder, humility, trust and love. (See Discussion Starters, page 86.)

The Communion Rite

As the last echo of our "Amen" sounds, we all stand. Some people pop right up. Others slowly, sometimes painfully, pull themselves to their feet. Children usually squirm a bit to loosen up. The Eucharistic Prayer is ended. Thus far we have followed the

Lord's example by taking and blessing the bread and wine. We still need to join in the breaking of the bread and the distribution of the bread and wine. We now have prayers to say and something to do. These challenge us to become conscious of the reality they symbolize. During the Eucharistic Prayer the challenge was to believe that Christ becomes present beneath the appearances of bread and wine. During the Communion Rite the challenge is to believe that by eating his body and drinking his blood we not only share in his divine life, both now and in eternity, but that we are also united to one another in a community of faith. We are affirming and strengthening our belief that as members of the body of Christ we share similar beliefs, that our ambitions and desires are going in the same direction, that we are willing to use our individual gifts for the benefit of others, and that we take personal responsibility for achieving the goals of the community. There is no doubt that many obstacles to this unity exist. Nevertheless, when we are fed at the table of the Lord we are called to recognize our oneness with all the other children of God. (See Discussion Starters, page 86.)

The Lord's Prayer

The celebrant invites us to join with him in praying as Jesus taught his disciples to pray. Our bodies join our words in this prayer. A uniform way of praying the Our Father has not yet been adopted by all parishes. We may simply fold our hands in a prayerful posture. We may join hands with those who are on either side of us. We may elevate our arms with our hands open and facing to heaven. One of the oldest pictures of a Christian praying has the man standing and extending his arms heavenward. This gesture carries many meanings. It is a sign of opening oneself to God, of begging favors from God, of greeting the Lord, of joy and anticipation. Each of us on any given day attaches our own sentiments to this gesture.

It is impossible to think of a Christian community which would not use the Lord's own prayer as a preparation for Communion. There is evidence that it was used in this way by some communities at least as early as the second century. We know for sure that from the sixth century it has been part of the community's preparation for Communion.

The acclamation, "For the Kingdom, the power and the glory are yours, now and forever," was added to our present Mass in 1969. This very old doxology, or hymn of praise, was a Jewish expression of praise that was used frequently by the early Christians. Very early in the East Christians concluded the Our Father with these words. Some of the scribes who copied the Bible were so accustomed to the liturgical use of this phrase that they added it to Matthew's words. We are used to thinking of these words as a Protestant ending, but they go back at least fourteen hundred years, before Martin Luther and his translation of the Bible. His and subsequent Protestant Bibles were translated from manuscripts into which these words had crept. The Vulgate translation of the Bible from Greek into Latin by Saint Jerome used a manuscript without the words. Today scholars agree that they are not part of the original text, but they are so meaningful and have such a long history that the Church has revived their liturgical use.

It is obvious why the Our Father is the perfect meal prayer said as a preparation for eating and drinking in memory of Jesus. In very concise words it lays out what we hope will come as a consequence of our partaking of the body and blood of Christ. We express our trust and hope that the kingdom of God, where his will is done, will evolve on this earth. In spite of all that we see and experience we have hope that all will become members of the community of faith. In the light of all that is going on in the world today this seems like a foolish dream, but as people of hope we trust that somehow and in some way it will come about. Implicit in this expression of hope is the realization that God works through human beings and that we are committing ourselves to the task of helping the world around us see what the Kingdom of God is like.

We ask for daily bread. This bread is not merely that which we put on the table three times a day. It is also the spiritual food we need in order to live a gospel life. It is a plea for everything we need to live a decent human life. It is not only a plea for this kind of food for ourselves, it is also a cry that all peoples will have enough bread on their tables, roofs over their heads and the other necessities of existence. In order to show that in some little way we are worthy to receive Christ, we tell the Father that we will forgive all our brothers and sisters just as he has forgiven us without any conditions or restrictions.

It seems that the secret of active participation at this time is saying the prayer slowly and reflectively. We are so familiar with the words that we tend to rattle them off without thinking too much about their meaning. Often someone with a strong voice will be racing through the prayer and those who wish to be more prayerful will seem to be dragging it. There is no way that we can rush the Lord's Prayer and still express the sentiments Jesus put into this prayer. If enough people recite the prayer with feeling and thought most likely in time the entire congregation will also slow up. (See Discussion Starters, page 86.)

Sign of Peace

The priest extends his arms in a collective embrace as he offers the peace of Christ to us. The peace which Jesus offered so frequently to those he met is the natural outcome of a faith which expresses itself in the Lord's Prayer. We accept the celebrant's wish and turn it back to him in our response. At his direction we turn to those near us and exchange the Sign of Peace. We usually shake hands, but we may kiss our spouse or our children. It takes but a moment to shake the hand of those in the pews near us, but the words and the gesture have a profound meaning. Peace is mentioned six times in the few short prayers between the Our Father and Communion. It is not the peace that results from an absence of conflict. It is the peace that comes from a feeling of security, trust and unity with one another. It is the peace which Paul at the beginning and end of his letters prayed would be in the hearts of his readers. It is a peace we can experience even when sickness or adversity overcome us. It is the peace we expect to have in the kingdom to come.

The gesture is one of greeting and of sharing. We are greeting Christ and all the members of his body when we extend peace to even one member of the community. We are reaching out to the Christ who lives in that person and who embraces all believers. Our handshake is a sign that the blessing given by Jesus to his disciples on Easter is our gift to share with one another. It expresses our union with one another because we become one by eating the same bread and drinking the same wine. It fulfills the Lord's command that if there is anything between us and our brothers or sisters we must make peace before we can honestly offer our sacrifice to the Father. It is a wonderful time for members of a family to forgive one another the little faults that harm the peace in a household.

The use of the greeting of peace goes back to the earliest times. Through the ages it has been placed at different points in the Mass. At one time it was situated between the Liturgy of the Word and the Liturgy of the Eucharist. Today it is seen as part of the preparation for Communion. It is a simple action in which we individually and as members of the Church ask for peace and unity within the Church and with the entire human family. It is a sign before we receive Holy Communion that we are united by mutual love in the body of Christ. It should be offered in a dignified manner to those who are nearby. It is not a time to greet friends whom we have not seen in a while. I once visited a church where the Mass stopped for ten or fifteen minutes while people roamed up and down the aisles kissing people and wishing everyone a hearty "hello." This stampede broke the sense of respect and awe enkindled by the Consecration as well as the peaceful sense of recollection in preparation for Communion. On the other hand, I have heard of people who have refused to exchange the sign of peace with those near them for some reason or other. They must have lacked a sense of peace and unity with their brothers and sisters in Christ.

As in all the other parts of the Eucharist our participation is not merely in the action we do, but in the meaning we put into that action. Even being at odds with one person takes something away from the sincerity of our gesture. (See Discussion Starters, page 86.)

The Lamb of God and the Breaking of the Bread

In some churches we remain standing until all have received Communion. In others we kneel. We either recite or sing The Lamb of God. Once again we ask the Lord for the forgiveness of our sins and for peace. This very short litany was introduced in the Mass by Pope Sergius I about A.D. 700. Meanwhile, the priest is doing the third action Jesus performed at the Last Supper. He is breaking the bread. If a large host is used the litany may continue to be sung until the celebrant is finished breaking it into pieces.

It takes a bit of imagination to see in our present thin wafers the bread Jesus used. The Jewish bread he broke was round—about the size of a plate—and thick as a finger. The priest uses a large thin wafer. He will first break it into two pieces, then break off a tiny corner and drop it into the precious blood. This breaking and intermingling goes back to early Christian times. Bread had to be broken into pieces if it was to be shared by more than one person, and the Gospel accounts mention that Jesus blessed and broke the bread with which he fed the multitudes. The early Church followed his action. Even after the introduction of individual altar breads the custom continued. Today it is still practical to break off a small piece from the large host in order to mingle it with the precious blood.

This action does not symbolize that the Lord's body and blood need to be reunited, but it symbolizes that after the Resurrection they are united and cannot be separated. If we receive only the sacred bread or only the sacred wine we receive Christ whole and entire.

Of course, over the ages people have attached symbolic meanings to the three particles of bread and the commingling of one of them with the wine. One such ancient symbolic understanding sees different stages of the body of Christ in the three particles. The particle dropped into the precious blood refers to the Body of Christ after the Resurrection. The one consumed by the priest refers to the Body of Christ on earth and the third one to the Body of Christ in the grave. This type of symbolism is not in favor these days. *The Sacramentary* attaches a much deeper and more personal symbolism to this rite. We who are many are made one in Christ by sharing in the bread of life, which is Christ. A sense of our solidarity and of our union with our fellow believers is a very important part of our preparation for receiving Holy Communion.

Communion

As the celebrant holds the host above the cup and proclaims, "This is the Lamb of God who takes away the sins of the world. Happy are those who are called to his supper," we humbly acknowledge that we are not worthy to receive the Lord and ask that we may be healed. We step into the aisle and begin to move forward toward the Communion station. Most people have their hands folded and their eyes centered on the hosts being distributed by a priest, deacon or lay minister. Often the choir will be singing an appropriate hymn to put us into a humble welcoming mood. If we know the hymn we should sing along. We are not on a solitary stroll to receive the Lord. We are part of a procession in union with our fellow believers. We are preparing together to receive the Lord.

In the past we knelt along the altar rail as the priest moved from person to person putting the host on each one's tongue. Now we come up one by one and receive the host in our cupped hands and, if we wish, we may drink from the cup. The manner of receiving Communion has changed over the ages. The present practice goes back to the earliest times. It was not until the ninth century that the practice of the priest putting the host directly into people's mouths was introduced as a sign of the holiness of the body of Christ and to avoid profanation. Two centuries later kneeling became the custom to emphasize the holiness and majesty of Christ and the respect due to him. Today the usual custom is once again to receive standing up. The custom of drinking from the cup had also gradually died out. It, too, has been restored, because Jesus told his disciples not only "to take and eat," but also "to take and drink" in memory of him. Some people still hesitate to accept the cup. The bread we receive does not look much like the bread on our tables and is too small to be a part of a meal. The wine we drink is barely enough to wet the tip of our tongues. Yet the reception of both is a much better sign of a meal than merely partaking of one or the other.

Standing to receive the host is as respectful as kneeling, if by the way we stand we communicate a sense of reverence and faith. Not much faith or reverence is shown if we amble up the aisle, our eyes roving over the scene, our hands dangling at our sides, and if we casually accept the host and give a perfunctory "Amen" to the invitation, "The Body of Christ." It is true that a person can come to the altar with all the signs of reverence and respect and at the same time be unbelieving or alienated from Christ. Usually, however, our demeanor reflects our inner attitudes and belief. A recent document from Rome urges the faithful to make some sign of reverence just before receiving the Lord. This can be as simple as a slight bow of the head. It need not be as obvious as dropping to both knees and bowing low.

The simple gesture of extending our hands, one hand under the other, is a sign of welcome and of our recognition of the majesty of Christ. One of the Fathers of the Church wrote that by this action we are making a tiny throne for our king. The simple "Amen" to the words of the ministers, "The Body of Christ," "The Blood of Christ," is an affirmation of belief in the real presence of Christ. It is a way of saying, "I do indeed believe!" Quietly and devoutly we return to our places in the pews.

Our tendency while we are approaching the Communion station will be to focus on our personal feelings and on our personal relationship with Jesus. But we are members of the People of God approaching a common table. We need to be conscious of this fact and sing together and even say a prayer for the others in line with us. The few minutes of silence we have when we are standing, sitting or kneeling in our pew after we have received is a time for prayers of thanksgiving, praise and petition. (See Discussion Starters, page 86.)

Concluding Rite

Just as we need a few minutes to prepare ourselves for celebrating the Eucharist, we also need a few minutes for a simple ceremony of dismissal. However, before the dismissal there usually is a time for the announcements. Some people think that the Mass is no place for these "commercials." But the entire eucharistic celebration has been an activity of the community. It is true that we might think of it only as a spiritual activity. In our personal life as well as in our community life there is no real division between spiritual and secular activities. In both we are seeking God and God is seeking us. Thus the announcements give us an opportunity to learn how and where we personally can join with some of our fellow believers in doing a work of the Lord.

The celebrant greets us a final time, catches our attention and blesses us. Then he sends us forth. It is to be hoped that we have changed a little by our active listening to God's speaking to us through the Scriptures and the words of the liturgy and by our efforts at inner participation in the mystery in which we have had a vital role to play. Someone has written that if we have not been changed by the liturgy, then our attendance at it has been a waste of time. This may be an exaggeration, but there is enough truth in it to make us ask each Sunday, "In what way do I need to open myself more fully to the action of the Spirit whom the Lord sends to us?"

As we exit the church our life in and with Christ really just begins. Now we go out to live what we have professed and to share what we have gained with others. The first challenge is whether we greet, talk with, even make eye contact with our brothers and sisters who have worshipped with us. The second is the consideration we show one another as we pull out of the parking lot. The third is what we will do before the next celebration of the Eucharist to bring Jesus' message of concern, peace and justice to those we encounter in our daily living. Amen! (See Discussion Starters, page 86.)

DISCUSSION STARTERS

- *What do you think the purpose of the collection is? What is it a means to?*

- *What do the bread and wine symbolize to you?*

- *When you hear the priest begin the Preface what thoughts come to your mind?*

- *How would you explain the difference between a Mass and a prayer service?*

- *In what way do you say that the Eucharist is different from an ordinary memorial service?*

- *Which of the Eucharistic Prayers do you like best?*

- *What would you say you are expressing when you say "Amen" at the end of the Eucharistic Prayer?*

- *What is your favorite petition in the Lord's Prayer?*

- *How do you feel about exchanging the Sign of Peace?*

- *In a few words express what you believe you receive when you receive Communion.*

- *When you leave Mass, how are you feeling? What are you thinking?*